GOOD
SCHOOLS

The Seattle Public School System,

1901–1930

GOOD
SCHOOLS

The Seattle Public School System,

1901–1930

BRYCE E. NELSON

UNIVERSITY OF WASHINGTON PRESS

Seattle and London

This book was published with the assistance of a grant from PEMCO
Financial Center to the Seattle School District History Trust Fund.

Library of Congress Cataloging-in-Publication Data

Nelson, Bryce Eugene, 1945–
    Good schools: the Seattle public school system, 1901–1930/Bryce
E. Nelson.
        p. cm.
    Bibliography: p.
    Includes index.
    ISBN 0-295-96668-8
        1. Public schools—Washington (State)—History. I. Title.
LA384.S4N45 1988   88-6916
371'.01'0979—dc19   CIP

To Bonnie, Karl, and Eric

Contents

Contents

Illustrations

All photographs were taken by Asahel Curtis.

Illustrations

High school life drawing class
Lincoln High School, orchestra
B. F. Day School, calisthenics
Queen Anne High School, girls' gym
Ballard High School, football club
Franklin High School, boys' soccer

Following page 116

Lawton School field trip
Main Street School, Japanese American students in traditional
      costume
MacDonald School, May Day celebration
Lincoln High School, senior play
West Seattle High School, senior ball
Ira C. Brown, M.D., giving a medical exam
Seattle Public Schools Clinic, dental operating room
Milk break
Children's Orthopedic Hospital, children with teacher
Boys' Parental School, students playing marbles
Girls' Parental School, students playing baseball
Broadway High School, chemistry class
Broadway High School, women's carpentry class
West Seattle High School, business machines class
B. F. Day School, students knitting
Adams School, flag salute

Acknowledgments

This book started one afternoon in 1975 in the basement of the Seattle Public Schools administration building. I had innocently asked directions to the archives and instead was shown piles of old boxes stacked high in a basement corridor. Within a few years that material resided in the new Seattle Public Schools Archives, and I was able to use the collection. Archivists Lucille Murray and Eleanor Toews provided outstanding assistance. Helping me make sense of these documents by teaching me their context were three University of Washington professors: Robert Burke (History), who guided me through the history of Seattle; and David Madsen and Charles Burgess (Education), who taught me the history of American education.

A dissertation does not normally get rewritten into a book without additional help. Paul Hoerlein (Seattle Public Schools) and Robert Tostberg (University of Washington) played key roles in establishing the Seattle School District History Trust Fund, which helped underwrite the publication of this book. A grant from PEMCO Finanial Center, in memory of founder Robert J. Handy, is gratefully acknowledged.

Finally, a major debt of gratitude goes to my wife Bonnie and our children Karl and Eric. Our boys have never known a time when I was not working on this project. I think they would have liked these schools.

GOOD
SCHOOLS

The Seattle Public School System,

1901–1930

Introduction

Imagine yourself attending grade school in 1915. You walk a few blocks from home to a new, landscaped brick building. On the playground you recognize many of the students, from the little kindergarteners to the big eighth graders. There are only about 400 pupils in your school, and you know most of them, having grown up in this neighborhood. Despite being in a big city, the school community is too small for you to spend nine years in anonymity. Teachers, neighbors, and students know you. The boundary between proper behavior and misbehavior is clear, and each is likely to be noticed.

In your grade school you try out new skills, using both your mind and hands. You learn to read and write, but you also learn to sing, play sports, garden, cook, use hand tools, and draw. You dance around the Maypole, build model sailboats, and help the younger children bake cookies. The consequences of success or failure at any of these are not great. If you can saw a board straight, it does not follow that you are headed for more shop classes and then the carpenters' union. If you cannot saw straight, you are not a school failure. Informal and extracurricular lessons are as important as those from the books: learn right from wrong, and act accordingly; take responsibility; cooperate; and be a healthy, productive citizen. After grade eight you will probably go on to high school. There the consequences of success or failure will be more serious.

Such grade schools were in fact built in Seattle from 1901 through 1917, the formative years for both the city and its public school system. By conscious choice, reaffirmed until the 1920s, the Seattle school system developed as small, neighborhood grade schools (kindergarten through grade eight) with class size around 35 pupils, and four-year high schools with class size around 20 pupils. In these grade schools, children could grow slowly into early adolescence. They were not tracked into different curricula based on ability. The schools were more interested in transmitting academic content, and developing intellectual skills, character, morality, and good citizenship, than in job preparation.

The Seattle schools developed as they did because one man, Frank B. Cooper, was superintendent during the district's transformation into a major urban school system, 1901–1922. When Cooper arrived in 1901, Seattle was a frontier seaport characterized by a sleazy reputation, a high rate of transience, and muddy streets. It numbered only about 80,000 people. Within a decade, Seattle had become a city known by many as a good place to settle down, raise children, and live well. This rapid change in image was tied in part to the remarkably good school system developed by Cooper, in cooperation with supportive school boards and a handful of voters.

Between 1900 and the American involvement in World War I, 1917–1918, Seattle could be characterized as a progressive city, echoing themes of progressive urban politics from throughout the country. What set Seattle apart, however, was that its progressive leaders shaped the patterns in housing, business, politics, and public works while their new city was being built. Seattle progressives spent their time building, not being thwarted by intransigent special interests. The new Seattle emerged from yesterday's woods, not as a city of tenements and factories, but as a commercial and residential city. The new neighborhoods were villages of single-family houses and paved streets, complete with new municipal water, sewer, and electrical systems, and parks, boulevards, libraries, and schools.

The school system was the key to Seattle's progressive era self-image. The quality of a public school system tells much about the importance of children in that society. By implication, it reveals how that society views its own future. Justifiable pride in an urban school system implies a widespread sense of hope for the future.

Schooling in Seattle ceased to be an informal, haphazard endeavor affecting only a few children and even fewer adolescents. Instead, it became a large, systematic endeavor used by many people, from

4

children to adults. Taxpayers spent considerable sums and expected a considerable return. Through a combination of factors—Cooper's long tenure, his progressive vision, supportive school boards, and the lack of obstacles (political, financial, and demographic)—Seattle became an outstanding national example of progressive era schooling. As such, it demonstrated what public schooling, in its origins as an urban mass institution, could accomplish.

A pattern emerged for school reform in midwestern and eastern cities during the early twentieth century: urban schooling was frequently imposed by an elite and was controlled by this elite for its own purposes. These reformers replaced a large, partisan, ward-based school board with a small nonpartisan school board, elected citywide. Control of schools was thus shifted from various social, economic, ethnic, and religious groups to an elite, whose members then created a professionally staffed bureaucracy to run the schools. Commonly these new board members, their superintendent, and the educational bureaucrats saw schooling as a tool for social control, especially of newly arrived immigrants, the poor, and the nonwhite.

That pattern does not explain the Seattle experience. Unlike school boards elsewhere, the Seattle board had always been small, elected citywide instead of by wards, and nonpartisan. Seattle school politics were dominated by the same kinds of upper-middle-class business and professional men who were also involved in other civic affairs. But such men did not join the board to use schooling as a form of social and economic control over working-class youth.

Although board members regularly defeated labor-union, Socialist, and prominent women candidates, most of the defeated candidates were in general agreement with the board progressives on the direction of schooling. The lawyers, doctors, and businessmen on the school board did not form a coalition with unions, Socialists, and women's groups. Instead, all shared a progressive vision of urban schooling. The challengers only occasionally elected their candidates, and they did not control the school board. Nonetheless, the unions, Socialists, and women's groups could each claim that the school system contained features very similar to what each advocated.

5

For Seattle's middle- and working-class parents, immigrants, and racial minorities, the public schools were important places. The citizenry was confident of the future, and creating good public schools was a high priority on the political agenda of otherwise disparate groups. The board regularly built substantial new buildings throughout the city, keeping grade schools as small neighborhood institutions. Superintendent Cooper hired experienced teachers from throughout the country. Together, the board and Cooper expanded the formal curriculum and promoted some progressive ways of teaching, seeking to match curriculum and pedagogy with the developmental needs of children and adolescents. The teachers shaped student behavior, asserting a strong sense of parental responsibility, and the board intervened in the lives of poor, dependent, or delinquent children with an extensive social welfare program. Seattle youths (and adults) responded by attending these schools in great numbers, with the percentage in attendance very high as compared with other cities.

In the early 1920s, in Seattle and elsewhere, serious questions were raised about the cost, scope, and purpose of this new institution of public schooling. Confidence in the future had been shaken by World War I, and the importance of children and schooling began to drop on the political agenda. In Seattle, ideological and fiscal conservatives challenged the leadership of those who had shared the prewar label of "progressive." After the "red scare" and the Seattle General Strike of 1919, the de facto coalition between progressives, Socialists, and labor unions was replaced by class-based hostility.

The new board reexamined most aspects of Cooper's now-tainted progressive school system, from its cost and organizational structure to its curriculum and pedagogy. To some conservatives, schooling was just another expense to be reduced on the bloated tax rolls. "Offer less, and do it cheaper," they exhorted. The tax-cutters saw no reason for Seattle's teachers to have small classes and high salaries. They wondered just how extensive the curriculum and extracurriculum should be, and whether night schools, special and remedial education, and social welfare services should really be the business of the schools. They were interested in "efficiency techniques" such as intelligence testing, ability grouping, and the creation of junior high schools. The ensuing political struggle for control of the board brought to a close the formative years of the Seattle public schools.

This, then, is the story of Seattle in its important years of growth, as seen from one perspective—the development of its public school system. If public schools symbolize a community's sense of confidence in its future, then progressive era Seattle was a supremely confident place. Its woods were cut, its canals dug, its hills sluiced down, its utilities installed, and its buildings put up to last. During the years 1900–1917, Seattle ceased to be a frontier town of muddy streets, cheap wooden buildings, and a large population of transients. Instead, it became a city in which the quality of urban amenities became important to most residents, with good schools at the top of the list.

1

New Schools in a New City, 1901–1911

Frank Cooper had never seen any place quite like Seattle when he arrived in 1901. Part of it was a tawdry seaport town, well known to sailors, unemployed loggers, and transient men. But an even larger part of Seattle was rapidly becoming a medium-sized, respectable city. Cooper watched the woods being cut and, in their place, neighborhoods being constructed with single-family houses. Within a few years, he saw reformers struggling to make city politics as proper as these new neighborhoods. Good-government groups, organized labor, Socialists, and assorted reformers all contended with the problems left behind by frontier capitalism. And Frank Cooper, the new school superintendent from the rural Midwest, had before him the extraordinary opportunity to develop a new urban school system, essentially unencumbered by the past.

Jere Frank Bower Cooper was a product of the nineteenth century (born 1855) and of small Illinois towns. He attended Cornell University for one year (1878–1879) before returning to the Midwest to begin his teaching career. In 1883 the twenty-eight-year-old Cooper became school superintendent at LeMars, Iowa. He remained until 1890. He then spent one year as a professor of pedagogy at the State University of Iowa. Between 1891–1899 he was superintendent of schools at Des Moines, Iowa. Then Cooper left the Midwest for good, becoming superintendent in Salt Lake City for two years, after which time he was hired by the Seattle school board for fall 1901.

Cooper's background was typical of late-nineteenth-century superintendents: native born, rural, Protestant, white, married, and with his job status deriving from performance rather than from university credentials. Historians David Tyack and Elisabeth Hansot de-

8

scribe such nineteenth-century school superintendents as forming an "aristocracy of character," and their twentieth-century counterparts as being "managers of virtue."[1] Cooper's lack of an advanced degree in educational administration and his cautious approach to "scientific management" would separate him from his younger colleagues. Cooper would make occasional forays into the world of the twentieth-century scientific managers—but he would never quite fit in with them.

Seattle is a twentieth-century city. It burned in 1889. It was promptly rebuilt, but by 1900 it was still hardly a city, having only about 80,000 people and a high rate of transience. By 1910, however, Seattle had 237,000 inhabitants and many of the amenities expected of a city. Seattle's rate of growth was startling.[2] So was its transformation from a rowdy frontier town into a bourgeois city. Most of Seattle's single-family neighborhoods, its architecture, basic utili-

1. See David Tyack, "Pilgrim's Progress: Toward a Social History of the School Superintendency, 1860–1960," *History of Education Quarterly* 16, no. 3 (Fall 1976): 257–300; and Tyack and Elisabeth Hansot, *Managers of Virtue: Public School Leadership in America, 1820–1980* (New York: Basic Books, 1982). Cooper fits their profile (p. 169) of twentieth-century superintendents, differing only by his lack of an advanced degree and his move away from his home area: "Superintendents in the twentieth century have almost all been married white males, characteristically middle-aged, Protestant, upwardly mobile, from favored ethnic groups, native-born, and of rural origins. Typically superintendents have had long experience in education, beginning their careers as young teachers, going on to principalships, and then becoming superintendents (in larger communities they often became assistant superintendents along the way). In disproportionate percentages they have been older sons in larger than average families. Mostly they remained in the same state for their entire careers as superintendents. They have been joiners, participating actively in civic and professional groups. Most of them picked up their advanced education while they practiced their profession, with long gaps of time between their academic degrees. They have been disproportionately Republican and have generally been moderate to conservative in their social philosophies."

2. See Alexander N. MacDonald, "Seattle's Economic Development, 1880–1910" (Ph.D. diss., University of Washington, 1959), p. 320: "In 1910, compared to the next five smaller and larger cities, Seattle had a larger percentage of population increase than any of them, 1890–1910. Its population increased from 3,533 in 1890 to 237,194 in 1910, an increase of 6,600%." Only six cities larger than 100,000 had doubled in population, 1900–1910. Seattle was one, having increased at the rate of 194%. See Ellwood Cubberley, *The Portland Survey: A Textbook on City School Administration Based on a Concrete Study* (Yonkers-on-Hudson, N.Y.: World Book Co., 1915), p. 94.

ties, public and private institutions, and its people were new in the early twentieth century.

One afternoon in Cooper's second year, a school board meeting was held on a board member's yacht. As they cruised Lake Washington, Cooper might have pondered the miles of undeveloped shoreline forming the eastern boundary of Seattle. The view from the yacht was of a forested region with enormous potential to become a major city. Cooper's task was to guide the development of a school system, keeping pace with the rapid transformation of those woods into neighborhoods.

The Seattle school system developed at a time when urban public schooling was being created as a large-scale institution throughout America. Across the nation, schooling was to change profoundly during the years between the turn of the century and the American involvement in World War I. As noted earlier, large urban school boards commonly became small nonpartisan groups of prominent men, elected citywide instead of by wards. In addition, school administrators organized their systems along hierarchical models used in the corporate and business world. Teaching became white-collar women's work, something educated people with teaching credentials chose for a career. Almost all children and adolescents began attending school, staying about nine months each year, and returning for more years than ever before. By World War I, adolescents customarily attended high school. This new enterprise of mass urban schooling cost a considerable amount of new tax dollars, reflecting progressive era transformations in urban politics, landscape, and institutions. New parks, libraries, water and sewer systems, paved streets, and public schools—all became important amenities in progressive American cities.

Frank Cooper and the Seattle public schools were local variants on these national themes. From its mid-nineteenth-century beginnings, the Seattle school board had always attracted financially comfortable and socially prominent men. They served on this unpaid board out of a sense of civic duty—and, depending on the perceived threat, to keep schools away from control of Populists, Democrats, Republicans, Socialists, or labor leaders. In 1888 the group had been enlarged from three members to five, elected citywide. Thus the board that hired Cooper was small, its members knew one another well, and they made efforts to keep things that way. Long time Board Secretary Reuben Jones recalled the "spirit of kindly fellow-ship that prevailed among members of the Board."[3] Very few people who did not travel in the social and economic circles of the board members ever came close to winning election or appointment. When a vacancy occurred, a peer was quickly chosen. The group watched out for itself.

Almost all school board members during Cooper's tenure (1901–1922) were white male Protestants, middle aged, born and raised elsewhere, well educated, socially prominent, financially comfort-able, and politically safe. These men had made their fortunes as Se-attle grew. Regardless of their professional backgrounds, most were also in real estate, insurance, or investments. Almost all had moved to Seattle as adults in the decade following the 1889 Seattle fire.

There were good reasons why the school board under Cooper was composed of people with so much in common. For one, school board members thought of themselves as nonpartisan in school af-fairs. That was self-deception, as more members over the years were Republicans than Democrats. More pointedly, the label "nonparti-san" meant they certainly were not candidates backed by organized labor, Socialists, ethnic, or tax-cutting groups, all of whose candi-dates were labeled "partisan." The *Argus*, a weekly downtown newspaper usually supportive of the "Business Men's Ticket," ac-knowledged this nonpartisan self-deception by editorializing:

> We claim that we have no politics in the public schools. As a matter of fact there is little of anything else. And the pathetic part of it is that the school directors and Superintendent Cooper do not real-ize it, and when they state that our schools are absolutely free from politics they tell the truth as they see it. But any institution de-pending on the suffrage of the people, and supported by taxation, .

3. Reuben Jones, Reminiscences, 1940, Superintendent's Papers, A78–15, Seattle Public Schools Archives (hereafter cited as SP).

which has so tight an organization that for many years it has been impossible for an outsider to break into the management, is in politics.[4]

Voting requirements effectively limited the kinds and numbers of voters. This also was a factor in creating board homogeneity. The handful of school supporters who made the effort to vote usually prevailed. The regular failure of labor to get out its voters underscored this. Socialists turned out regularly, but there were not enough Socialists to win without a coalition.

In 1904 school elections were separated from the November general election and were held on the first Saturday in December. A winter Saturday election ensured a low voter turnout, so annually a handful of school partisans passed bond levies and elected likeminded school directors. Starting in 1904 women could register separately and vote in school elections. That resulted in even more proschool votes for incumbent board members and their colleagues.[5]

School board elections commonly received very little advance newspaper publicity. Voters got the word about elections and candidates from school-related networks: parents' groups, women's clubs, civic associations, business groups, and churches. The "right" people knew about school elections; the majority either did not know or did not care. Taking school elections out of partisan politics meant that the few who voted could usually elect a peer of the existing board. But, as the newspapers regularly reminded, voter apathy could also result in an organized group's electing its candidate—especially the Socialists.

Another reason the Seattle school board attracted like-minded members was economic. One needed a measure of independence

4. *Argus*, November 11, 1911, p. 4.

5. As examples of low voter turnout: in 1904, 18,087 voted in the November 8 general election, but only 3,704 (including women) voted in the December 3 school election. About 1,200 Socialists voted in each election. The winning candidates received 2,593 and 2,622 votes. *Seattle Times*, November 9, 1904, p. 1; ibid., December 4, 1904, p. 3. In 1910, 23,117 voted in the November 8 general election, but only 3,606 in the December 3 school election. The Socialist candidate received 406 votes. *Seattle Times*, November 9, 1910, p. 1; ibid., December 3, 1910, p. 1. Seattle's population in 1910 was 237,194.

12

from job demands to find time to attend to board business—as elsewhere, school board members were unpaid volunteers. In Cooper's first decade, none of the members was short of money, and none was from the working class. Almost all members were self-employed professionals, such as lawyers or doctors, or were prominent businessmen. That remained true throughout Cooper's tenure, and was typical nationally of progressive era school board members.[6] From the ranks of upper-middle-class business and professional men came those who saw to it that schools, parks, libraries, sewers, water mains, and streets were built.

Logical candidates for the board would have been socially prominent married women who were financially comfortable and therefore had time to spend on school business as unsalaried directors. During Cooper's tenure, women ran in fourteen elections, and one-fifth of the candidates for board seats were women, including five with impressive backgrounds. Only Anna Louise Strong was elected, however, and only with the help of organized labor. The business of the board was not perceived as women's work.

The board's self-image was that of men running a rapidly expanding business. Board meetings were dominated by selling bonds, retaining the district's credit rating, taking bids for new construction, letting contracts, suing contractors, buying books and supplies, and haggling with teachers over salaries. Curriculum, pedagogy, and personnel were left to Cooper. Anna Louise Strong recalled of her time on the board:

> Questions of education they never dealt with; they referred them
> to the superintendent. The interest of the board members was in
> gas and heating contracts, new buildings for important new areas,

6. The only Socialist elected to the board, Richard Winsor, was a lawyer. He noted that the board had met 102 times in 1913 and concluded: "A poor man or a man of ordinary means could not make the sacrifice to be a member of the School Board. He would have to be a person of ample means on the one hand, or semi-retired like myself, on the other" (*Seattle School Bulletin*, December 1913, p. 2). Of the largest 46 cities in the United States, only 7 had paid school board members in 1916, and this pay was minimal. See *The Public School System of San Francisco, California* (Washington, D.C.: United States Commissioner of Education, 1917), p. 81; Scott Nearing, "Who's Who on Our Boards of Education," *School and Society* (January 20, 1917), pp. 89–90.

the spending of public funds. For me those sessions were the most completely boring hours of my existence, spent in long debate over various makes of electric switches or plumbing fixtures, with never a word on the aims or methods of education.[7]

This acted as an effective sieve in determining who got elected.

In Cooper's first year as superintendent, the board at one meeting authorized purchase of "colored cardboard for weaving."[8] This inconsequential purchase was representative of hundreds of similar details dealt with by this board of prominent, successful men. In 1902 the board could spend its time voting on every nickel and making petty decisions alongside major ones. It is almost a surprise to note how many outsiders to the business world wanted to join this board, knowing that the board's time would be spent mostly on business-related items.

One such attempt made by outsiders for a board seat occurred in 1905, when some German-Americans ran a candidate. The German-Americans made the only ethnic attempt during Cooper's tenure to gain a school board seat—and it was a clear failure. In Seattle, ethnic politics was not part of school board politics. The *Argus* earlier had noted: "When they hold the right of franchise they are Americans. . . . It is time to set down on people who claim to be able to deliver the colored vote, the Irish vote, the German vote, or the Scandinavian vote. These men are too intelligent to be voted like cattle."[9] Seattle before 1910 had relatively few immigrants, and of those, many had learned American ways in previous cities. School politics was remarkably free of appeals based on political party, class, ethnicity, race, or sex, even though it would have been feasible to win with an organized bloc because of low voter turnout.

7. Anna Louise Strong, *I Change Worlds: The Remaking of an American* (Seattle: Seal Press, 1979), p. 52.

8. Minutes of Board, February 7, 1902.

9. *Argus*, November 8, 1902, p. 2; Janice Reiff concludes about immigrants and Seattle: "It was not the place in which immigrants learned the American language or American customs, it was the place in which they put into practice all the American ways they had learned along the way to Seattle." Janice L. Reiff, "Urbanization and the Social Structure: Seattle, Washington, 1852–1910" (Ph.D. diss., University of Washington, 1981), p. 225.

No organized bloc could overcome the widespread perception of the Seattle school board as the place for businessmen who knew how to construct buildings. This perception matched the way the board members spent their time. As hard-nosed businessmen, they tried to get full value for every dollar. They regularly denied extensions to contractors who could not finish work on time, did not hesitate to sue contractors over shoddy work, and rejected all bids for work if none seemed low enough. As an example of the board's hardheaded business ways, it decided in 1903 to withhold for six months half of the payment on a contract to fix the roof at Webster School, "to give time for a thorough test of the work." Sometimes getting "full value" for the dollar meant being "not fancy." The board rejected bids for a railing in the superintendent's office and instead directed that "a plain, simple railing be constructed."[10] Remarkably, there were no financial scandals. Each year the books were audited and judged clean.

From the late nineteenth century, the board did its real work and made its decisions in subcommittees of three members. Requests from individuals or groups commonly came to the board in writing rather than in person, and the requests were routed to the appropriate subcommittee for a recommendation. In these closed-door subcommittee meetings, Cooper and the board members learned to know one another well as they debated and made district policy. Subcommittee decisions were then routinely approved with very little discussion at board meetings.

Even a small district required support staff, both for the board and for building-level work. Most of the new staff worked on maintenance and construction of facilities, not on administration related to teaching. These people commonly served "at the pleasure of the board" and were dismissed when not needed. The school board clearly was not creating a permanent bureaucracy but simply was hiring people to help with bricks-and-mortar problems.

It was expensive to realize the vision of schooling promoted by Cooper and the board. To hire new teachers and build schools necessitated raising large sums of tax money. "Efficiency" was a key word

10. Minutes of Board, June 8, 1903 (Webster); ibid., December 8, 1902 (railing).

for progressive schoolmen, but "efficient" did not mean "cheap." The board raised and spent considerable sums, and while they watched every nickel, they built buildings to last and they supported programs that required more staff.

School revenue was raised through property taxes. The 1891 Washington state legislature had authorized school districts to collect a five-mill property tax. An additional tax of up to ten mills could be levied if voters approved. In 1909 the legislature raised the limit to ten mills without a vote, and an additional twenty mills with a vote. Each year during Cooper's twenty-one years in Seattle, the voters approved an excess-bond levy. The vote was rarely close. Indeed, Seattle residents voted to tax themselves for both civic and school improvements at a rate that made Seattle's per capita bonded indebtedness among the highest in the nation.[11] This was an expression of an ability to pay, of confidence in the future, and of a shared vision for the quality of Seattle's urban life.

By the end of Frank Cooper's fifth year in Seattle, a pattern had been set for the next decade. Seattle was quickly becoming a new twentieth-century city, growing at one of the fastest rates in the nation. While Seattle had comparatively few children, the percentage of children attending school was near the top nationally. And Seattle was near the top in per pupil spending on schooling. Cooper's immediate concerns were all directly related to managing the rapid growth of the system. The district was relatively successful at keeping up with the enrollment demand. The system gained students as the city annexed land, and for a variety of reasons (including the 1903 compulsory law), most children started to attend grade school, and many went on to high school. Cooper and the board responded by building many small neighborhood grade schools (instead of fewer large ones). They built comprehensive high schools, but no junior high schools. The board also tried to keep class size among

11. Seattle's per capita bonded indebtedness for all civic purposes was $134.27, second highest cited, well above the average of $96.20. For schools, the indebtedness was $15.66, third highest, with the average at $12.40. See *Public School System of San Francisco*, p. 147.

the smallest in the nation—under 35 pupils per class in grade school, and about 20 in high school.[12]

The neighborhood grade school played an important part in Seattle's transformation from a rowdy frontier town full of transient single men, to a home-owning, settled, middle-class city. Much of this new city was composed of distinct neighborhoods, for which the central institution was the local grade school. The neighborhood grade school stood for stability, neighborliness, and the assumption that the upcoming generation could be educated, socialized, and turned into responsible citizens. None of this had characterized Seattle's immediate past.[13]

12. For comparative data on growth, school attendance, and spending, see Ellwood Cubberley, *School Organization and Administration: A Concrete Study Based on the Salt Lake City School Survey* (Yonkers-on-Hudson, N.Y.: World Book Co., 1916), p. 10; idem, *The Portland Survey*, pp. 93, 94, 102; *Public School System of San Francisco*, pp. 22–27. On compulsory school attendance, see *Laws of Washington*, 1903, 55, chap. 48, March 7. Determining class size is difficult because of overcrowding in parts of the city and annual variations in enrollment, and because Seattle offered many special education classes and had auxiliary teachers. Grammar school class size commonly was 30 to 35, high school around 20 (with many classes below 20). Compared with other cities, these figures were quite low. A 1913–1914 report of the United States Commissioner of Education listed Seattle's average number of pupils per teacher in the grades at 31.6, and high school at 19.8. In a memorandum about this table, Cooper asserted that higher class sizes "would be contrary to well advised public policy and insupportable to the people of this city." Frank Cooper, Memorandum to School Board, March 2, 1916, SP, Folder "Report of State Examiners." In a 1919–1920 study of 169 cities by the New York City Chamber of Commerce, Seattle ranks very high on attendance, class size, and teacher preparation. See "Efficiency of Seattle Schools," SP, Folder "Seattle Schools Statistics."

13. Seattle had a comparatively high percentage of single men, who usually resided south of downtown. Each winter the lack of work in lumber, fishing, and farming caused even more single men to migrate into Seattle (Robert Saltvig, "The Progressive Movement in Washington" [Ph.D. diss., University of Washington, 1967], p. 420. Reiff, "Urbanization and the Social Structure," shows that by 1910 the new family neighborhoods were built for people of "similar economic status, wealth and ethnic origin" (p. 167), and that "local institutions such as churches and schools reinforced these tendencies" (p. 215). These new neighborhoods were of single-family houses, and hence Seattle had a comparatively high percentage of home-owners (43.4%). See *United States Census*, 1910, vol. 1, p. 1366. Indeed, the degree to which Seattle was developing as a collection of neighborhoods concerned civic-minded leaders, who saw strong neighborhood loyalties working against citywide solutions to

The presence of a neighborhood school now conveyed a message of hope for the future, a reassurance that through these schools Seattle would become a civil city. The school building was also the symbol of community identity and cohesion. Even people who did not have children in school cared about the appearance and reputation of their neighborhood school for reasons related to real estate values and neighborhood identity, or because this grade school was also the community center.

The physical appearance of a school building was important to the board and to community boosters. The board built buildings well, often of brick. For example, in the winter of 1908 the board directed architect James Stephen to draw two sets of plans for a new school, one set for a brick building and one set for a wooden frame building. The brick school cost 22 percent more, but board members chose to build of brick.[14] They were building schools to last.

Through substantial school buildings with landscaped and well-maintained grounds, the board made a statement not only about the importance of schooling in the present development of Seattle but also about the long-term connection between schooling and the kind of city it hoped Seattle would become. Its actions reflected the advice in a pamphlet on school landscape, issued by the county school superintendent, advocating that schools "be a model in appearance, surroundings and neatness of upkeep for the homes of the community."[15] The board spent money for landscaping, concrete sidewalks, flowers, and shrubs—and for gardeners to take care of it all.

Maintaining the appearance of school grounds was an important expression of a middle-class neighborhood. Each summer the dis-

---

problems of rapid growth. The Municipal League was started in 1910 as a group for those with a citywide agenda. Lee Pendergrass notes: "The common perception among reformers was that neighborhood consciousness was unusually pronounced because the topographical peculiarities of the city (its hills, valleys, canals, and lakes) divided it into a number of more or less isolated geographical districts which lacked any sense of community or common identity." Lee Pendergrass, "Urban Reform and Voluntary Association: A Case Study of the Seattle Municipal League, 1910–1929" (Ph.D. diss., University of Washington, 1972), p. 10.

14. Minutes of the Board, February 10, 1908.

15. James E. Gould, *Planning and Improving School Grounds* (Seattle: County Superintendent of Schools, 1916), p. 2.

trict went to the expense of watering school lawns rather than letting them dry out. It planted flowers around schools and successfully encouraged neighbors to do likewise. In 1909 the district bought 800 dahlia bulbs, divided them among the schools, and asked that "patrons of schools be solicited to supply an equal number of bulbs for their respective schools."[16] Clearly, when a district invites residents near a school to donate flower bulbs—and the residents do so—the school as an institution plays a remarkable role in the life of a neighborhood.

Strong neighborhood identification with a grade school helps explain why so many grade schools were built. Seattle was overwhelmingly a city of single-family houses, and neighborhoods had natural geographic boundaries of hills and water. People had strong attachments to their neighborhoods, and the schools were central to that feeling. In 1914 Board Secretary Reuben Jones noted that the locations of the schools were "apparently very satisfactory to school patrons—complaints as to distances to school being exceedingly rare." Of the sixty-four grade schools, forty could be enlarged. Seattle grade schools averaged 440 pupils, while Census Bureau statistics for cities the size of Seattle showed an average of 532 pupils. Jones concluded that "hence possibly we have been rather liberal in the number of buildings."[17] The board's decision to build many small grade schools—and to keep them small—was not due just to geography. It was a conscious policy decision based on the kind of schooling perceived as most desirable for children and young adolescents.

On several occasions the board created controversy over school name changes—further suggestive of neighborhood identification. In 1903 the board decided to rename almost all schools. The new names were to come off nationally circulated lists known as "American Immortals" and the "Roll of Fame." The public's reaction was negative. In a remarkable bow to community-based pressure, the board rescinded the new names in the fall of 1903. Again in 1908 the board backed down on school name changes, keeping the neighbor-

16. Minutes of the Board, February 26, 1909.
17. Reuben Jones, Memorandum to School Board, May 12, 1914, SP.

hood names. When Cooper retired in 1922, fifty-six of the sixty-nine grade schools were or had been named for their locations. Throughout Seattle there persisted a strong identification between a neighborhood and its grade school.

Community groups in Seattle wanted access to "their" school buildings during nonschool hours. Prior to Cooper, the board had rented school rooms to groups for meetings. In November 1901, because of requests for use of rooms by Sunday schools, churches, and neighborhood improvement clubs, the board decided "not to grant the use for any other purpose of rooms regularly used by the schools, and to rescind all permits previously granted." In response to protests, the board reaffirmed that "school buildings be used only for purposes directly connected with school work."[18]

In 1910 Cooper again urged increased community use, saying that "the schoolhouse when used by the people for the discussion of public and social questions becomes in a new and very vital sense the seat of influence for the maintenance and perpetuation of free institutions." He urged that every school be built with an assembly room, accessible from the street, so it could really be the center for all kinds of neighborhood group meetings. In 1911, under further prodding from the Municipal League, the board ended its lingering opposition to community use of school buildings and formally approved use of schools for "civic and neighborhood meetings of the proper kind."[19]

Neighborhood adults received permission to use schools as community centers, but children had a harder time gaining permission to use school grounds as play space. Seattle schoolmen were ambivalent about providing space for unsupervised play, expressing concern about cost of acquiring land, legal liability, and miseducation on unsupervised school grounds. And they were not interested in supervising play after school hours, something they understood to be the job of park-department employees.

Sandlots, playgrounds, and parks were built in late-nineteenth-century cities to keep children off the streets, lower the juvenile

18. Minutes of Board, February 17, 1902.
19. *Annual Report*, 1910–1911, p. 32 (Cooper); Minutes of the Board, January 9, 1911 (board).

Frank Cooper, superintendent of the Seattle Public Schools, 1901–1922, guided the district through its transformation into a large, progressive urban school district. (*Seattle Public School Archives*)

Board of Directors, Seattle Public Schools, 1910. Top row, left to right: Ebenezer Shorrock, Edmund Bowden, Reuben Jones, secretary. Bottom row: Frank Cooper, superintendent, Everett Smith, John Schram, William Pigott. (*Seattle Public School Archives*)

Warren Avenue School, recess, 1905. (*Washington State Historical Society*)

School district architect's office, 1909. The school district employed its own architect (James Stephen, Edgar Blair, then F. A. Narramore), who kept busy drawing new buildings and enlarging old ones. (*Washington State Historical Society*)

Warren Avenue School, teachers eating lunch, 1905. Grade school teachers were usually female, well educated, un-married, and had recently moved to Seattle from the Midwest or East Coast. (*Washington State Historical Society*)

Longfellow School, arithmetic lesson, n.d. Progressive era pedagogy featured "learning-by-doing" activities, such as this arithmetic lesson in which students are weighing and measuring objects. (*Washington State Historical Society*)

Summit School, kindergarten, n.d. After 1912, the Seattle schools began establishing kindergartens throughout the city. (*Seattle Public School Archives*)

West Queen Anne School, class, n.d. Children learned about nature, drawing, and carpentry by studying birds and building birdhouses. (*Washington State Historical Society*)

University Heights School, model sailboats, 1910. Manual training in grade schools was designed to make students familiar with hand tools, not to be pre-apprentice training for only certain students. (*Seattle Public School Archives*)

Pacific School, history class, n.d. Progressive-era study of history featured activity-learning as well as reading, seat-work, and recitation. (*Seattle Public School Archives*)

West Queen Anne School, auxiliary teacher, n.d. Most grade schools had an auxiliary teacher who worked with small groups of either remedial or advanced students. (*Washington State Historical Society*)

Lincoln High School, chemistry lab, 1909. Lab science was part of the liberal arts curriculum offered to all high school students. (*Washington State Historical Society*)

High school domestic science class, 1926. (*Seattle Public School Archives*)

Broadway High School, wood shop, n.d. All Seattle high schools were built as comprehensive high schools, complete with extensive shop facilities. (*Seattle Public School Archives*)

Broadway High School, auto shop, 1917. (*Seattle Public School Archives*)

Broadway High School, foundry, n.d. (*Seattle Public School Archives*)

crime rate, and provide healthy play space. Sandlots, playgrounds, and large wooded parks each had different intended functions, but all were part of a larger movement to bring rural amenities to cities Prominent landscape architectural firms, such as Olmsted Brothers, were creating the park systems of Chicago, Minneapolis, and Seattle (1903). Similar efforts were underway in many other rapidly growing cities. Urban land was being set aside for play (sandlots, playgrounds, and beaches), beauty (boulevards), and education and wildlife (forest preserves). But for children and youths, the issue was not preserving urban forests for "open space" or aesthetic "appreciation." The issue was creating play space in developed neighborhoods.[20]

From early in the century, the school board tried to buy extra land for school grounds. At the same time, it did not intend to provide playgrounds for the city. In 1903 the board endorsed the campaign of the Seattle Federation of Women's Clubs to have the city council acquire and maintain playgrounds. The board viewed this as a way of escaping pressure to use school grounds for unsupervised play during nonschool time.

In 1908, exploring its institutional boundaries, the board considered extending the hours of its responsibilities by "caring upon the school premises after school for the children of parents compelled to work through the day." Educators were concerned that unsupervised children were more liable than not to have miseducative experiences when a parent was not home. The board subsequently decided not to provide after-school day-care. Instead, it encouraged the park board to staff playgrounds for such a purpose.[21]

In 1909 the county prosecuting attorney issued an opinion that "the board was not empowered to make expenditures for supervision and care of playgrounds except as incidental to care of school property etc." The board's attitude toward school grounds as public playgrounds turned decidedly negative. It even banned ball-playing

---

20. See Dominick Cavallo, *Muscles and Morals: Organized Playgrounds and Urban Reform, 1880–1920* (Philadelphia: University of Pennsylvania Press, 1981); see also *A Seattle Legacy: The Olmsted Parks* (Seattle: Seattle Department of Parks and Recreation, 1981).

21. Minutes of Board, August 14, 1908.

on school grounds on evenings and weekends. Nevertheless, the Seattle Play Ground Association continued to urge the board to buy land adjacent to schools for playgrounds. In a policy switch, the board sought and received voter approval at the December 1910 election for $100,000 for school playgrounds, with many neighborhood groups petitioning for one.[22]

All of this support for playgrounds during 1910–1911 brought a negative reaction from the Principals' Advisory Committee—which was "unalterably opposed to allowing people to congregate on the school grounds or about the building, or having the grounds used as public playgrounds, without proper supervision."[23] School principals would bear the burden of solving problems of vandalism and violence on the school grounds. Teachers and principals alike would be inconvenienced when windows were broken. Nevertheless, the board bought land, and these new school grounds were used as play space during and after school.

The uppermost concern of the board during Cooper's first years was space—buying enough land and building enough schoolrooms to keep up with the enrollment. Compared with most growing cities, Seattle's board was remarkably successful. Cooper's direct concerns were with personnel and curriculum. Not only did he personally hire hundreds of new teachers, but under his guidance the curriculum was expanded greatly and the way in which students were taught was altered. These changes in curriculum and pedagogy followed trends occurring elsewhere and were commonly cited as characteristics of progressive era education.

22. Ibid., August 9, 1909; ibid., May 9, 1910; ibid., November 7, 1910.
23. Ibid., June 16, 1911.

2

Expanding the Curriculum, 1906–1911

Frank Cooper inherited not only an uneven collection of school buildings but also a curriculum in need of change. And change was in the air, promoted most notably by the writings of John Dewey. While Frank Cooper did not attribute his educational philosophy directly to Dewey, many changes he advocated between 1906 and 1911 were in the direction suggested by Dewey and other "pedagogical progressives."[1] The board let Cooper, its hired expert, set the agenda for educational change. Under his leadership, the formal curriculum of academic work was greatly expanded in both grade and high schools, and the traditional textbook and recitation method of teaching was altered by new teaching techniques. Cooper's significant curricular and pedagogical changes were rarely discussed by the board and were hardly noticed by the public.

What is immediately striking about the formal curriculum of the grade schools is the remarkable variety of subjects studied and experiences made available to the students. The traditional curriculum of science, mathematics, language, and history was greatly expanded under Cooper, starting with a major curriculum revision in 1906. New subjects were added, so that most Seattle grade schools offered music, art, physical education, manual training, domestic science, and gardening. Student governments and newspapers were

---

1. The term "pedagogical progressives" is used by David Tyack in *The One Best System: A History of American Urban Education* (Cambridge, Mass.: Harvard University Press, 1974). He distinguishes those progressive era educators interested in curriculum and teaching methods from their contemporaries, the "administrative progressives," who were more interested in reorganizing school administration (pp. 180–98).

started. Elaborate pageants and musicals were produced, capped by an all-city music festival in the spring.[2] In short, there was plenty of activity learning to help balance the traditional passive book work.

Themes from John Dewey were evident here and there, perhaps best summarized in Dewey's observation that education "is a process of living and not a preparation for future living." Dewey recounted an incident which captured the spirit of the new pedagogy. While unsuccessfully trying to find suitable school tables and chairs, Dewey was told by a furniture dealer: "I'm afraid we have not what you want. You want something at which the children may work; these are all for listening."[3] In that spirit, one Seattle grade principal observed about the changes being made: "With the aid of pupil cooperation we have tried to change some of the cold, stern features of the school, to the freer ideas of the Houses of Childhood, and we like it."[4]

The curriculum was essentially standardized throughout the city, with lesson guides, and suggested activities, and all promoted by subject matter supervisors who went from school to school, and even held Saturday teacher meetings. End-of-the-year examinations from the supervisors were given to all students from the fourth grade onward who had averaged less than 80 percent on their class work in a particular subject. Final grades and promotion were based on a combination of teacher-made tests given throughout the semester, and, as a "quality control" check for those who had not done well, a standardized examination.[5]

The curriculum was the means by which Cooper tried to shape a unified system from the semi-autonomous buildings he had inherited. Through lesson guides, meetings with supervisors, and observation by principals, the teachers not only knew what to teach but

2. On June 16, 1915, a Department of Music was established. Within a year, 28 grade schools had orchestras. See *Annual Report*, 1915–1916, pp. 123–24. Vocal music flourished during World War I, promoted by 9 supervisors from the Department of Music.

3. John Dewey, *My Pedagogic Creed* (New York: E. L. Kellogg & Co., 1897), p. 7; idem, *The School and Society* (Chicago: The University of Chicago Press, 1900), p. 47.

4. *Annual Report*, 1912–1913, p. 45.

5. Frank Cooper, Bulletin to Principals, June 2, 1908, SP.

how to teach it—and, in some instances, even when to teach it. This centralized persuasion was focused on promoting the new progressive curriculum and pedagogy.

Defining how progressive curriculum and pedagogy actually looked in a classroom was as hard then for educators as it is today for historians. It is especially awkward to use the term "progressive" over several decades, or to compare classrooms of small, experimental, progressive private schools with those of large urban public-school systems. Historian Larry Cuban outlines a definition with which pedagogical progressives early in the century would have agreed. This consensus includes:

> instruction and curriculum tailored to children's interests; . . . instruction to occur as often as possible individually or in small groups; . . . programs that permitted children more freedom and creativity than existed in schools; . . . school experiences connected to activities outside the classroom; . . . children [encouraged] to help shape the direction of their learning.[6]

Except for the last point, classroom-level curriculum and pedagogy in Seattle before World War I actually went in these directions. Such classroom-level changes made Seattle stand out from most other districts, where, as Cuban shows, progressive rhetoric seldom produced classroom change. A number of classroom-level examples will suggest the direction taken in Seattle toward progressive curricular and pedagogical goals, 1906–1911.

The grade school curriculum featured many activity or nonbook kinds of learning. For example, students did physical exercises during school, but not in a required gym class. Cooper did not want formal gym classes, especially for elementary school children, observing that "play and free outdoor exercise greatly transcend systems of gymnastics in the development and fostering of physical vigor and health."[7] Teachers showed children some games, then let them play.

6. Larry Cuban, *How Teachers Taught: Constancy and Change in American Classrooms, 1890–1980* (New York: Longman, 1984), p. 44.
7. *Annual Report*, 1909–1910, p. 28.

The only problem Cooper saw with this informal playground time was that the older girls stood around too much. He observed that "their lack of physical vigor is too often due to lack of opportunity to take this kind of exercise." Hence, Cooper often sought ways to get these young adolescent girls to exercise. On one occasion he advocated building a tennis court at each grade school, observing that "tennis is a sport that should be encouraged by the school authorities because it is a recreation that can be carried through life, and it is the aim of the gymnasium to establish habits that can be practically carried on in later life and make for greater health."[8] The board, however, chose not to build tennis courts at grade schools, although they did so at the high schools.

Manual training in the grade schools was also part of the formal curriculum. Advocated by the Federation of Women's Clubs, manual training was started by the board in five grade schools in 1903–1904. The following year, sewing and cooking were added for seventh and eighth grade girls. Manual training was not vocational, job-oriented training, although familiarity with tools could be considered preparation for vocational training in high school. Manual training students learned to use hand tools and made small projects. This was close to John Dewey's ideas about broadening the school experience of children through handwork, and then connecting handwork to other subjects studied or to the child's home life.[9]

Cooper described the goal of manual training in grades four through eight as enabling a student to "acquire skill, power to create, and appreciation of construction work in the world about him." When the manual training boys at Beacon Hill and Whittier Schools built additions to their school shops, Cooper praised them not only for the "experience of actual construction" but because "they had civic and social experiences which were made to function vitally all through the work."[10]

8. Ibid., 1910–1911, p. 27; ibid., 1913–1914, p. 89.

9. See Dewey, *The School and Society*, especially chapter 6, "The Psychology of Occupations" (p. 131): "The fundamental point in the psychology of an occupation is that it maintains a balance between the intellectual and the practical phases of experience. . . . Occupation as thus conceived must, therefore, be carefully distinguished from work which educates primarily for a trade."

10. *Annual Report*, 1909–1910, p. 24; *Quinquennial Report*, 1916–1921, p. 75.

Cooper promoted a variation on manual training which had a big impact on older grade school students. Starting in 1911–1912, three grade schools offered a new two-year course called "Industrial Training." Like manual training, industrial training did not have a vocational end. Cooper said this new course was aimed at students who "fail to get in the grammar grades the best kind of preparation either for further study or for self-support and independent citizenship that they are capable of receiving."[11]

The industrial training students divided the day between academic and shop work. The academic work was concentrated, and Cooper did not think they suffered: "Some pupils at least have done better work than they have ever done before." For the first year, students were referred because they were doing poorly in their schoolwork and were a grade or more behind their age. They began the program as children "lacking habits of study, and accustomed to failure." Cooper later confessed they "presented problems both in instruction and discipline that taxed the resources of their teachers." But "by the end of the year the classes had achieved a decided success," and parents gave a "practically unanimous endorsement of the work."[12]

The industrial training classes allowed Seattle to resist the national trend toward junior high schools. Most American school systems were organized with eight-year grade schools and four-year high schools. Then, starting with junior high reorganizations in 1909 in Berkeley, California, and Columbus, Ohio, some districts began to reorganize so that grades seven, eight, and nine were in a separate building. The junior high school quickly gained adherents because of new interest in what were perceived to be unique needs of the age group. Psychologist G. Stanley Hall's *Adolescence* (1904) was widely popular among educators. The new junior high schools were designed to respond to differing student needs by offering academic or prevocational courses, thereby sorting young adolescents into educational and job tracks. In addition, and equally important, junior

11. *Annual Report*, 1911–1912, p. 26.
12. Ibid., 1912–1913, p. 33; ibid., 1911–1912, p. 27; ibid., 1912–1913, p. 33; ibid., 1911–1912, p. 27.

high schools were hailed as a less expensive way for school districts to cope with burgeoning high school enrollment.[13]

In Seattle, Cooper preferred keeping seventh and eighth graders in small neighborhood grade schools, where faculty and neighbors knew them well, and where students could try shop classes without being tracked into a vocational course. In listing disadvantages of a junior high school, Cooper cited teaching by subjects, which not only "increases the number of teachers for each individual pupil and decreases the amount of personal attention and care" but also "increases the tendency to specialization on the part of teachers and deification of the subject."[14]

Cooper concluded that between ages thirteen and sixteen, some prevocational study was desirable for the general education of all. He thought a boy should "study concretely some of the practical problems derived from a fundamental productive industry or occupation that is locally important." Further, he thought a girl could profit from home economics rather than the "almost exclusive book study . . . for it transfers the questions with which she is asked to deal from hypothetical or distant situations to the sphere of the actual and near." Neither Cooper, the parents, nor the children considered industrial training to be preparation for a specific job. Rather, it was a way to increase the interest, ambition, and industry of young adolescents. In 1914–1915 Cooper noted that eleven industrial training centers were scattered around the city "without reference to class or neighborhood distinctions."[15]

Art and music were also integral parts of Cooper's new grade school curriculum—they were not frills tacked on later. Each was promoted by a supervisor. Art consisted mainly of drawing, with supplemental craft projects. Music consisted of group singing and, usually, a school orchestra. Many rooms were equipped with pianos.

---

13. See Thomas H. Briggs, *The Junior High School* (Boston: Houghton Mifflin Co., 1920), p. 30. See also Joseph K. VanDenburg, *The Junior High School Idea* (New York: Henry Holt & Co., 1922); Leonard V. Koos, *The Junior High School* (New York: Harcourt, Brace & Co., 1921).

14. *Seattle School Bulletin*, April 1919, pp. 2, 3.

15. *Annual Report*, 1913–1914, p. 47; ibid., p. 46; *Annual Report*, 1914–1915, p. 62.

Still another nonbook part of the grade school formal curriculum was the school garden program. Garden work started in 1911 at the urging of the local Congress of Mothers and Parent-Teacher Associa tions. Grade school students planted gardens at school and at home. Several high schools had botany classes and greenhouses. By 1915 school gardening had become so popular that a supervisor was appointed. Students not only grew vegetables, but older students were instructed in pruning and grafting apple trees and rose bushes. At three schools in poorer neighborhoods, rose bushes were sold at cost to students to plant at home. Often students were mobilized and went throughout a neighborhood destroying tent caterpillars or earwigs. There was constant praise for the school garden program.[16]

Gardening was justified because it taught students responsibility, taught scientific knowledge of plants, promoted cooperation between home and school, beautified a neighborhood, saved money in families that grew vegetables, gave children wholesome work to counteract "the influence of the street," and perhaps even led to employment for some students. Cooper liked all the lessons that could be taught through gardening: "The child studies THINGS, not through the eyes of the writer of the text books, but through his own." One teacher described gardening as "school work . . . just as is arithmetic, history, geography, drawing, music or any other study—and the gardening is made a study, a garden-school."[17]

Compulsory attendance laws, the emergence of educational psy-

16. On the origins of gardening, see Frederick Lash, "An Historical and Functional Study of Public Education in Seattle" (Ph.D. diss., University of Washington, 1934), p. 295. See *Annual Report*, 1914–1915, p. 57 (supervisor); Charles C. Gray, Memorandum to Frank Cooper, February 15, 1915, SP, Folder "School Gardens" (pruning). Regarding students destroying caterpillars, one principal wrote: "They went about the work of destruction so effectively as to thoroughly clean the district of this pest" (*Annual Report*, 1912–1913, p. 43). In the spring of 1921 the schools organized a citywide campaign against earwigs. Cooper applauded such campaigns, noting "the ethical and social value of such work cannot be over estimated" (*Quinquennial Report*, 1916–1921, p. 78). See also *Seattle School Bulletin*, January 1921, p. 4, for a summary of how schools organized campaigns against caterpillars and earwigs.

17. *Quinquennial Report*, 1916–1921, p. 77 (gardening justified); Frank Cooper, Memorandum to School Board, April 7, 1915, SP, Folder "School Gardens."

chology, an expanded curriculum, and the tremendous increase in the number of students—all resulted in the schools' interest toward children not considered "normal." In Seattle, academically talented students were promoted ahead of their age group but were not placed in a special program with their peers. Children who were deaf, retarded, physically handicapped, delinquent, or overage for their grade level, or who had speech, learning, or behavior disorders—all were given the choice of attending the "special education" class created for them, or of staying at home and not attending the local school.[18] These special education classes were usually held in one room in a building, and were dispersed among many buildings. The state compulsory attendance law exempted those with mental and physical disabilities from attendance in regular or special education classes. Those of low mental ability, however, could choose to attend the Child Study Laboratory at Cascade School or the Olympic School for "sub-normal children." Serious cases of delinquency were sent by the juvenile court to the school district's parental schools. And, starting in 1912, a teacher was assigned to the Children's Orthopedic Hospital.

All of the above special education programs were similar to those of other urban school systems prior to World War I. They were created not only in response to students with special needs who now appeared at the school door, compelled by new laws to attend institutions they had previously avoided. In addition, progressive era educators actively sought ways to reorganize the school experience to attract students with special needs. Such educators believed that very few children had needs beyond what the school could provide. Even for those few, they believed appropriate custodial institutions could be created, such as local parental schools for delinquents, or state boarding schools for the retarded. Seattle was sometimes in the vanguard of districts creating special education programs, sometimes in the ranks. Its overall special education program was exemplary without being unique.

While separate classes were established for those students with a variety of learning problems, the district also provided extra help to

18. Minutes of Board, January 11, 1911.

students who were unable to keep up in their studies, or who were exceptionally bright and could go ahead in their work. Starting in 1909, this extra help was given by auxiliary teachers. An auxiliary teacher worked in a grade school as the faculty member with flexible time to meet building needs. Who and what these women taught was determined at the building level, a reminder that the district was not a centralized bureaucracy. Sometimes auxiliary teachers did small-group tutoring or divided a class with the teacher. This program ended the practice of putting all low-achieving pupils of a building in one room. Now these students stayed with their regular class and were periodically called out for tutoring by the auxiliary teacher. By far the most time was spent on arithmetic. And by far the most children helped were those doing poorly rather than those who were advanced. Sometimes auxiliary teachers made home visits, often making referrals to the psychological and medical clinics. The program started with three auxiliary teachers in 1909 and expanded quickly to thirty-five in 1912–1913. A *Seattle School Bulletin* article concluded:

> The auxiliary system in Seattle is probably unlike that of any other city. In some school systems the auxiliary teacher is a special teacher of music or drawing, in others the principal's assistant. In no system have we found the auxiliary teacher so largely the central factor among all school agencies that can be utilized to the advantage of exceptional children.[19]

In 1911–1912, with new goals for history and geography, grade school teaching techniques continued to move away from recitation, rote memorization, and seat work. A new "project-problem" method was introduced to teach pupils to reason and to "socialize and develop power in oral exposition," instead of just repeating answers. A generalized statement was given to a student to prove. This required using various sources, determining relevant parts of the proof, and organizing a convincing talk. Cooper asserted that

19. *Annual Report*, 1912–1913, p. 30 (arithmetic); ibid., p. 31 (remedial students); *Seattle School Bulletin*, May 1915, pp. 1, 4.

"in the upper grammar grades there are many boys and girls who can reason closely enough to arrange related facts in well-connected paragraphs, make a brief outline, and then stand before the class and talk in a pleasing and convincing manner."[20]

Cooper acknowledged opposition to the project-problem method by critics who charged that "the grammar school is no place for research work, debate and discussion of opinion." But he dismissed such criticism, claiming that the statements given students to prove were not controversial and that the "research" was hardly rigorous. Cooper also admitted that students taught in this method did poorly on the citywide examination, which was still geared to rote memory of facts. That caused more criticism of the project-problem method.[21]

A poor showing by eighth graders on an American history examination brought the question of pedagogy out in the open between Cooper and at least one board member. Hermon W. Craven wanted to improve test scores. He wanted Cooper's progressive pedagogy replaced by traditional teaching, using one textbook, with emphasis on drill and memorization of names, dates, and facts. Cooper stood by the new method and said those teachers who used it "deserve special commendation." Cooper thought that improving test scores would come at "too great expense." He wanted young adolescents to learn how to learn ("to employ books of reference intelligently and usefully"), and to like to learn (to create a "taste for a noble and inspiring study"). "The school that turns out pupils long on dates and facts," he wrote, "and short on interest in history and in the relation of events has failed signally." In a phrase capturing the spirit of progressive era pedagogy, Cooper told his critics: "I question the advisability of deifying mere memory and fact-getting." One principal supported Cooper by attesting to the good results of the problem method: "The timid boy and girl are gaining confidence in themselves and strength in expression." Another praised its beneficial effect on the teacher, changing the role from that of "dogmatic and dictatorial questioner." The project-problem method remained.[22]

20. *Annual Report*, 1912–1913, p. 34.
21. Ibid., 1912–1913, pp. 36–46.
22. Ibid.; Hermon W. Craven, *Report of Hermon W. Craven on the Teaching of United*

Not only was the grade school curriculum expanded to teach children by using more activity learning, but the high school curriculum underwent a profound shift. Traditionally, high schools had offered one "common core" liberal arts curriculum to all, but very few adolescents had stayed in school. In the early twentieth century, however, the high school curriculum was greatly diversified, so that by the 1920s high school was attended by most adolescents.

Two important national reports demonstrate a fundamental shift in character and purpose of the high school curriculum throughout America in these years—the 1894 Committee of Ten *Report* and the 1918 *Cardinal Principles of Secondary Education*.[23] The Committee of Ten *Report* outlined past and current practice by suggesting that a student follow one of four curricula: Classical, Latin-Scientific, Modern Languages, and English. These four courses of study actually had much in common. Each was, in effect, a modern liberal arts curriculum. Each was considered suitable as preparation for college or, if a terminal degree, as preparation for life.

Twenty-four years later, the *Cardinal Principles* advocated specialized courses, to be organized by job categories and offered in a comprehensive high school. The cardinal principles as such were: health; command of fundamental processes; worthy home-membership; vocation; citizenship; worthy use of leisure; and ethical character. These principles were translated into specific high school courses of study (or tracks), which did not necessarily share much in common with one another. High schools were becoming mass institutions, with preparation for specific jobs and life roles seen as the socially efficient use of the high school.

These nationwide trends also affected Seattle high schools. During Cooper's tenure, attendance increased explosively, and the high school curriculum changed from a common course for all to differen-

States History in the Grammar Schools (Seattle: Board of Directors, Seattle Public Schools, 1913), pp. 22–26.

23. Committee of Ten on Secondary School Studies, *Report* (New York: National Education Association, American Book Company, 1894); Commission on the Reorganization of Secondary Education, *Cardinal Principles of Secondary Education* (Washington, D.C.: Government Printing Office, 1918). See also Theodore Sizer, *Secondary Schools at the Turn of the Century* (New Haven: Yale University Press, 1964).

tiated tracks.[24] Seattle's 1907 "Course of Study" listed the following options: classical; Latin; modern language; history; science; manual training; commercial; and art.

Cooper was not happy with high school solely as preparation for college. He wanted teaching to be influenced by the needs of developing adolescents, not by college standards. He observed: "Probably the most nutritive high school instruction, considering the residuum of usable material left with the pupil, is in those departments where the teachers are least influenced by college standards." Most students were not going to college, hence, Cooper did not want to see students founder or be forced out of high school because the curriculum and teachers were geared only to the college-bound.

Cooper also advocated that teachers of ninth and tenth grade students teach two subjects to the same students rather than specialize in only one subject. "It is better," Cooper thought, "for a pupil to have only two teachers for the four subjects he carries and to have those teachers know him well, and feel greater responsibility for him and him to feel greater responsibility in his class relations, than for him to meet daily four specialists who, because of the number of different students they meet every day, can scarcely be expected to know and meet individual claims upon the personal side."[25]

An important part of expanding the curriculum was deciding whether to have all courses offered in all high schools (a "comprehensive" curriculum), or to have some high schools specialize. This was a bricks-and-mortar decision, settled as each new high school was built prior to World War I. The question raised was how extensive should each school's shop, home economics, and commercial

24. Cooper's first year, 1901–1902, there were 872 high school students, with 92 graduating. Cooper's last year, 1921–1922, there were 10,885, with 1,506 graduating.

25. *Annual Report*, 1909–1910, p. 33. In a report on his visit to the Gary, Indiana, schools, Cooper noted that Gary high school teachers "are become instructors in subjects rather than teachers of boys and girls—that the subject becomes the end rather than the instrument and that the personal element becomes too nearly submerged. It is at this point that the high school everywhere breaks down, particularly in the first and second years and it is for this highly important reason that I am trying in our own high schools the plan of reducing the number of teachers a boy or girl may have in order to make the personal touch more decided and responsibility more clear" (Frank Cooper, Letter to William Pigott, February 26, 1915, SP, Folder "Vacation").

programs be? Several times it was proposed to have Broadway High School specialize as the school for vocational, technical, and home economics education.[26] Such specialization was rejected, and each high school continued to offer a comprehensive curriculum.

Nationally, the nature and scope of vocational education was the central question in transforming high schools into mass institutions. In a comprehensive high school, the "common school" ideology (i.e., a common curriculum shared by students of all racial, ethnic, and socio-economic backgrounds) was altered to include different courses of study for students whose interests, abilities, and anticipated occupations required training in other than the traditional liberal arts. Thus, trends in the marketplace determined the need for work-related education and helped to determine which students would take which classes.[27]

In Seattle, all the various shop, cooking, sewing, and commercial classes were offered in all the high schools throughout the city, rather than being concentrated in only a few schools, or requiring students seeking such training to attend one school. Whether in grade or high school, offering shop, home economics, and commercial classes was considered beneficial for all students, not just those from working-class neighborhoods. While most girls took home economics, and many boys took shop, the popular classes were commercial—typing and stenography for girls, and bookkeeping for both boys and girls. Seattle was a commercial rather than a manufacturing city. Office jobs were available, especially for young women.[28]

26. Minutes of Board, January 27, 1908; ibid., July 8, 1914. See also *Annual Report*, 1911–1912, p. 5.

27. See Marvin Lazerson and W. Norton Grubb, *Vocationalism and American Education: A Documentary History, 1870–1970* (New York: Teachers College Press, 1974); John L. Rury, "Vocationalism for Home and Work: Women's Education in the United States, 1880–1930," *History of Education Quarterly* 24, no. 1 (Spring 1984): 21–44; Edward A. Krug, *The Shaping of the American High School*, (2 vols.; New York: Harper & Row, 1964, 1972); Harvey Kantor and David Tyack, eds., *Work, Youth, and Schooling: Historical Perspectives on Vocationalism in American Education* (Stanford: Stanford University Press, 1982).

28. See MacDonald, "Seattle's Economic Development, 1880–1910." Compared with ten cities of similar population, manufacturing in Seattle in 1910 was a small part of the economy (12%). MacDonald concludes (p. 328), "Practically all of the goods manufactured in Seattle were prepared for use in the city itself or else helped meet the

The needs of the marketplace attracted many Seattle students to these commercial classes.

Another new part of the comprehensive high school curriculum was physical education. After several years of informal classes, compulsory noncredit gym classes were required for all freshmen and sophomore students in 1910–1911 at Broadway, Queen Anne, and Lincoln High Schools. All had to take a physical examination before starting the class. Cooper claimed this "radical departure" of giving physical examinations was "well received," as it "gave the girls an opportunity to talk over physical matters with the director."[29]

Cooper was convinced that gym class was important to adolescents, especially to girls. In 1911–1912, one-half credit was given for gym class each semester, something Cooper thought "added energy and enthusiasm, particularly in the girls' department." When parents requested that a child be excused from gym, Cooper advised "for the best interests of their children such requests should not be entertained." Cooper liked the results of gym class, noting "straightened shoulders, better poise, clearer eyes and firmer handclasps from those who seemed to have a weak hold on life."[30] To further encourage physical activity among high school girls, the schools sponsored fall and spring Saturday hikes of four to ten miles.

In addition to expanding the curriculum in grade and high schools, Cooper established a parallel system of night schools which offered classes to adults, foreigners, and working youth. Cooper's vision of schooling was that of a social agency embracing almost all ages and attempting to meet a variety of needs—kindergarteners would play, and adults take vocational classes; juvenile delinquents could be reformed, and hospitalized children taught; foreigners should be naturalized, and racial minorities educated. The school

---

needs of the lumbering, mining, fishing, and agricultural industries in the Puget Sound area." Seattle was, instead, the financial and commercial center of the Pacific Northwest. See also Cubberley, *The Portland Survey*, p. 103, for a chart showing Seattle's low percentage (4.2%) of population engaged in manufacturing compared with similarly sized cities.

29. *Annual Report, 1910–1911, p. 29.*
30. *Ibid., 1911–1912, p. 34; ibid., 1910–1911, p. 28; ibid., 1911–1912, p. 35.*

was to be open days, nights, and summers. It was to be the symbol of community cohesion as well as the actual agency promoting community cohesion. Young and old, normal and deviant, rich and poor, American and foreigner—all could be part of the Seattle school system.

Adults with a variety of educational needs—from grade school to vocational classes—looked to the free public night schools. Night schools in Seattle made a modest beginning on January 6, 1902, operating for three months. In 1906 an evening high school opened, with the district attempting to offer each course taught in the day school. By 1908 the Seattle night school had grown to over 3,000 students registered, although it was always plagued with a high rate of absenteeism and attrition. It operated for six months each year, offering grade school, high school, and vocational classes. There was no tuition, nor were there age restrictions. Cooper noted: "If a man is never too old to learn, he is never too old to attend school."[31] Night school was clearly everybody's second chance at schooling.

Offering free night school to adults was but one more example of the extensive and expensive changes brought about by Cooper. And, as demonstrated by school board politics and the number of children, adolescents, and adults who attended classes, this school system was widely supported. The business and professional men who normally held board seats continued to be elected. Ethnic groups, organized labor, Socialists, and prominent women were unable to elect one of their own, partly because their platforms were not significantly different from what the schools were already doing. And the voters always approved the excess-bond levies, an indication of approval for the direction set by Cooper and the board.

Ethnic and racial groups made little attempt for a board seat, with the only challenge coming from German-Americans in 1905. Ethnicity was not a big factor in Seattle city or school politics. This was probably because Seattle had relatively few immigrants, most of whom had some money and were "Americanized." Also, immigrants lived throughout the city rather than in ethnic neighborhoods. The largest immigrant groups in Seattle during the Cooper

31. *Quinquennial Report*, 1916–1921, p. 63.

years were from Canada, Norway, Sweden, England, Japan, and Germany. There were relatively few people (about 4 percent) of minority racial backgrounds living in Seattle, 1900–1922. The largest group was of Japanese background, followed by blacks and Chinese.[32]

If ethnic and racial groups seldom attempted to gain a board seat, other groups were quite active, notably the Socialists, organized labor, and club women. The annual attempts by Seattle Socialists to gain board seats reflected attempts by Socialists throughout America to influence public schools. Socialists were concerned that child labor, hunger, and poor health would keep working-class children from attending school successfully. They maintained that the development of a child was the responsibility not only of parents but also of society. Hence, Socialists supported attempts by schools to intervene in and improve the lives of young children. Socialists supported free textbooks and such school social welfare services as free milk, lunch, and medical care. They admired the pedagogical orientation of John Dewey and wanted to replace teacher-centered instruction with activity learning, so that working-class children could learn to control their own affairs and destinies rather than be dependent in an authoritarian world. Socialists wanted schooling to include industrial education for all, rather than for only the lower classes.[33]

32. For information on immigrants in Seattle, see Calvin Schmid, *Social Trends In Seattle* (Seattle: University of Washington Press, 1944), p. 98; see also Reiff, "Urbanization and the Social Structure: Seattle, Washington, 1852–1910." Enrollment figures for Japanese, black, and Chinese students can be found in each *Annual Report*, starting in 1909–1910. For example, in 1900 there were 2,990 Japanese, 406 blacks, and 438 Chinese in Seattle, with all racial minorities being 4.8 percent of the population. In 1910 there were 6,127 Japanese, 2,296 blacks, and about 900 Chinese, with all racial minorities being 4 percent of the population. In the Seattle schools during 1909–1910, there were 287 Japanese, 208 black, and 80 Chinese students out of an enrollment of 31,376 students. By 1920 the 7,874 Japanese in the city were 2.5 percent of the total population, and the 2,894 blacks were 1 percent of the population. The schools in 1919–1920 enrolled 892 Japanese, 301 black, and 185 Chinese students out of a total enrollment of 42,615.

33. See Joseleyne S. Tien, "The Educational Theories of American Socialists, 1900–1920" (Ph.D. diss., Michigan State University, 1972).

To prevent a Socialist from winning a Seattle board seat by default because of voter apathy, the newspapers regularly waved a "red flag" to get out the middle-class vote. They also neglected to print the names of the Socialist candidates. A front-page *Seattle Times* headline just before the 1906 election proclaimed: "NO INTEREST IN SCHOOL ELECTION. Apathy Is Menace to Seattle's Schools. Indifference of General Public to Annual Election Makes It Possible for Socialists to Win Tomorrow. Businessmen Do Not Show Interest." Such rhetoric appeared annually, especially in the *Times*, the newspaper characterized by Socialist Harvey O'Connor as "the mouthpiece of the Chamber of Commerce, the waterfront interests, and ultra-conservative Republicanism." When Socialists ran well, the *Times* said their high percentage was due "almost entirely to the apathy with which the issue was regarded by conservative men." The Socialists were perceived by the downtown newspapers as outsiders who not only were theoretical, unbusinesslike, bad for the city's credit rating, and radical, but who wanted to experiment with un-American ideas on an American institution.[34]

Superintendent Cooper and the prewar boards were not as hostile to the Socialist platforms as the waving red flag of the *Times* would suggest. Although no one would openly have admitted it, Superintendent Cooper, the boards, the moderate socialists, the trade unionists, and the club women actually shared similar goals for the Seattle schools. Socialists and labor made no alliances, public or private, formal or informal, with the school board. Nevertheless, while remaining socially apart, the progressive board and superintendent advocated much of what Seattle Socialists and labor wanted in the schools. That such disparate groups tacitly agreed on the nature of schooling was not unique to Seattle. Socialists, trade unions, women's reform groups, and elite school board members in varying

34. *Seattle Times*, November 30, 1906, p. 1; ibid., December 4, 1904, p. 3; Harvey O'Connor, *Revolution in Seattle: A Memoir* (New York: Monthly Review Press, 1964), p. 27. The *Seattle Times* objected to the Socialists because "they are, as a rule, theorists, whose theories are not balanced by practical knowledge of and experience in business affairs. . . . [If the Socialists win] news will spread abroad that Socialists are gaining control of the city and the city's credit will be considerably damaged" (December 2, 1904, p. 14).

degrees pursued similar school goals in some other cities, notably in Milwaukee, Kansas City, Rochester, Toledo, and Atlanta.[35]

The chief differences in Seattle between the board and its challengers centered on the degree and rate of implementation. The board moved more slowly than Socialists wanted, reflecting a desire by school patrons to have the kinds of schools Cooper was building without being taxed too heavily. Indeed, the Seattle board spent the prewar years trying to do much of what the Socialists advocated, but not because the Socialists had pressured them successfully. Buildings and playgrounds were added at a remarkable pace; a school medical and dental clinic was opened; community groups gained access to school buildings for after-hours meetings; teachers' salaries were raised; the sex differential in salary was ended; free and reduced-price milk was distributed; night schools were expanded greatly; and three kindergartens per year were built after 1912. Such items did not come from the agenda of revolutionaries. Harvey O'Connor described these Seattle Socialists, even the radical "reds," as "solid burghers, with rose gardens around their homes and a stake in the community."[36]

Organized labor also pursued school board seats, but despite its strength in Seattle (including a newspaper, the *Seattle Union Record*), labor never elected a member from its ranks to the school board. The Seattle labor movement was closely tied to the Socialists. Contrary to the advice of Samuel Gompers and the American Federation of Labor (AFL), Seattle labor believed that cooperation with Socialists and involvement in union political elections would not hurt the cause of trade unions. Labor and the Socialists played two roles in Seattle school politics: both groups pushed the board on interests of working-class children, and labor pushed the board to do business only with union firms—or at least to pay union scale.

35. See William J. Reese, " 'Partisans of the Proletariat': The Socialist Working Class and the Milwaukee Schools, 1890–1920," *History of Education Quarterly* 21, no. 1 (Spring 1981): 3–50; idem, *Power and the Promise of School Reform: Grass-roots Movements during the Progressive Era* (Boston: Routledge & Kegan Paul, 1986). See also Paul E. Peterson, *The Politics of School Reform, 1870–1940* (Chicago: University of Chicago Press, 1985).

36. O'Connor, *Revolution in Seattle*, p. 20.

Given the amount of building, it was inevitable that the board would deal with the relationship between public money and the labor-union movement. Should public money be spent to support organized labor by doing business only with union contractors? Should public money avoid union contractors? Or, as trustees of public money, should the board always look for the best value (i.e., usually the lowest bidder) regardless of whether the workers were union? A basic reason labor wanted representation on the board was to see that public money for construction went to union men. At the least, they wanted to make sure that public money was not used to oppose organized labor. The newspapers perceived labor's attempt to win board seats as a "partisan" threat. "Trade unions should not control the schools, any more than should any political party," pronounced the *Argus*.[37]

In Seattle, the school board platforms of Socialists and labor commonly advocated the same goals, in some instances using the same phrases. The points of agreement in their platforms give a good idea of what those outside power thought schooling should do. The 1910 labor platform is representative:

1. Enough school buildings to be built to accommodate all. Ample playgrounds, baths and gymnasium. Free medical attendance. School buildings to be open to public assemblages when not otherwise in use.

2. Fewer pupils to each teacher and more and better-paid teachers.

3. Teachers' tenure permanent during efficiency.

4. Women teachers to be paid the same salary as men teachers for the same work.

5. Compulsory attendance of all children under fifteen.

---

37. *Argus*, December 7, 1907, p. 1. An editorial in labor's newspaper, the *Seattle Union Record*, stated labor's concern: "Practically all the school buildings erected in Seattle during the past year were built by scab labor. The union label is tabooed by the present school board for the very reason for which we desire its use, and they hold that it is not 'business' to insist on union labor in the building of school houses when a contractor, by the employment of scab labor, can underbid a contractor who employs union labor" (December 5, 1908, p. 1).

6. Free meals and free clothing, if needed, to keep children from the necessity of work.

7. Night schools in every ward to accommodate those deprived of an early education.

8. Greatest attention to be paid to the lower grades.

9. Free kindergartens for all children between five and six years of age.

10. A general scientific, industrial, and physical education guaranteed to every child.[38]

Union men were satisfied with the education their children received. They saw no advantage to getting union men elected and gaining control of the board. Unions were not able to rouse their members on school issues to get their candidates elected. One school issue that could have interested union men (but did not until the Smith-Hughes Vocational Act of World War I) was control of the vocational training curriculum. Nor were union men interested in electing school board directors pledged to raising taxes for higher salaries to teachers, especially since the teachers themselves were not interested in becoming unionized. For union leadership to attack schools that the rank and file found satisfactory would have weakened the credibility of union leaders.

The most serious challenge for a board seat came not from the Socialists, not from labor, but from the women's suffrage groups. Despite being able to vote in school elections since 1904, few women did. The *Argus* smugly claimed that women were "fairly well satisfied with the manner in which schools are run," and so "they do not care to vote." In 1909, however, women almost elected Mary Elizabeth Bettinger, a prominent club woman and civic activist. The *Times* was not amused by the serious challenge of the suffragettes, calling Mrs. Bettinger an "ambitious woman politician" and remind-

38. *Seattle Union Record*, December 3, 1910, p. 1. Socialist platforms were very similar. The 1912 Socialist platform added two items that never occurred in labor platforms: "We favor the employment in every school attended by girls of a qualified woman to act as a school matron"; and, "We demand that pupils be instructed in the principles and doctrines of universal peace, and that the Boy Scout movement and all other forms of militarism be discouraged" (*Seattle Times*, December 6, 1912, p. 12).

ing its readers that "experiments are dangerous. If the people want a safe and sane administration they should rally around Smith, Bowden and Pigott." In her 1909 loss, Mrs. Bettinger received 630 votes, while one board member was elected with only 849 votes. Mrs. Bettinger lost again in 1910. Seattle was a city of a quarter-million population, but because of low voter turnout, not many votes were needed to win. Nevertheless, it was hard even for organized women's groups to get the necessary votes.[39]

After 1910, women could vote in Washington in all elections, and they did so in significant numbers. Despite this, another prominent woman, Dr. Maud Parker, was defeated in the 1911 school election. Her strong effort, however, helped elect the first Socialist to the board, Judge Richard Winsor. Winsor, a semiretired attorney and former Michigan judge, also received many women's votes and won the third seat in the election. The confident incumbents, Edmund Bowden and Ebenezer Shorrock, refused to campaign actively. Low voter turnout, combined with strong efforts by Socialists and women, resulted in Judge Winsor's victory. The *Times* had tried its best to counter voter apathy by waving the red flag, proclaiming that a Socialist might get elected. Despite the warning, only 9 percent of the registered voters turned out. Shorrock observed in disgust, "The lightness of the vote makes one pause and consider seriously whether it is worth while to make the sacrifices that are too little appreciated."[40]

Although prominent women could not get elected to the board, society women nevertheless had the easiest access of any group to the prewar board. The Seattle Federation of Women's Clubs regularly presented requests to the board. In 1903 the Federation worked to create Parent-Teacher Associations throughout the city. In 1909 Cooper formed an advisory committee of club women, "to connect the superintendent closely and vitally with the home view and feel-

39. *Argus*, December 12, 1908, p. 1; *Seattle Times*, December 4, 1909, p. 1 (Bettinger election). In 1904, only 151 women registered to vote in the school election. In 1906, 540 women registered, and in 1907, 1,027 women registered, although not all actually voted. In 1909, the vote totals were: Edmund Bowden, 1,730; William Pigott, 1,647; Everett Smith, 849; Mary Elizabeth Bettinger, 630.
40. *Seattle Times*, December 3, 1911, p. 19.

ing." They lobbied for such issues as kindergartens, housekeeping rooms, a school for wayward girls, and school savings banks.[41] The board used no other community or civic groups as a regular sounding board. The Congress of Mothers and Parent-Teacher Associations made occasional statements to the board. Despite not being able to get one of its members elected, the Federation of Women's Clubs had more direct influence on the board than had the teachers, the Municipal League, organized labor, the Socialists, political parties, city government, the churches, or the chamber of commerce.

By the end of Superintendent Cooper's first decade, the Seattle schools had been changed dramatically. There were now sixty-seven school buildings, most of them less than ten years old, with more on the way. The curriculum had been greatly expanded for both grade and high school. To a degree rarely seen in other cities, progressive teaching methods shared time with traditional recitation and book work. Special education classes, auxiliary teachers, and night school now were available to those with special needs.

Throughout this transformation in scale and purpose, Cooper had remained a strong believer that the quality of a school system was determined by the quality of its classroom teachers. New buildings, curricula, and methods were important, but only if the right people were hired to teach. And that was Superintendent Cooper's responsibility.

41. Prominent women who ran for the school board and lost were: Mary Elizabeth Bettinger, Dr. Maud Parker, Nellie Burnside, Dr. Lilian C. Irwin, and Evangeline Harper. See Minutes of Board, March 12, 1913; ibid., March 26, 1913. On origin of PTA, see Lash, "An Historical and Functional Study of Public Education in Seattle," pp. 289–93.

3

Teaching as
an Emerging Profession,
1910–1911

Ten years after Frank Cooper had arrived in the rough port town of Seattle, it had begun to look like a middle-class city. Seattle by 1911 had a quarter-million inhabitants, property owners had bonded themselves heavily for urban amenities, and most residents lived in neighborhoods of single-family houses. Seattle looked like a good city in which to settle down and raise children.

But it took more than substantial-looking school buildings, complete with flowers and playgrounds, for citizens to consider their schools "good." Residents cared about who was teaching and what was taught. The reformist school board that hired Frank Cooper was determined to end political patronage in teacher hiring. Hiring was to be based on competence. When they hired Cooper, the board adopted three rules that left no doubt about reforms to be made under the new superintendent:

> 1. The sole purpose of the public schools is education. No other question will be considered in the appointment of teachers.
> 2. The purpose for which the schools are established is not to furnish employment for teachers. All teachers must possess high personal character, liberal education and strong bodily health.
> 3. Successful experience must be demonstrated. Professional training in the principles and practice of teaching is demanded. The use of personal or political influence to secure employment, or the request for the appointment of a teacher as a personal favor to anyone will not be permitted.[1]

1. Minutes of Board, May 7, 1901.

Superintendent Cooper took these statements seriously. Beginning with his first year, Cooper paid close attention to the personnel of his system. Indeed, Cooper viewed the major part of the superintendent's job as hiring teachers, providing leadership and guidance on what and how to teach, and serving as teacher advocate to the board. It appears that Cooper hired teachers on the basis of educational background, successful teaching experience, letters of recommendation, and a personal interview when possible. Additionally, all teachers needed to be certified (a combination of coursework, teaching experience, and a city or state certification examination), and, after 1915, to pass a physical examination.

Throughout his tenure, Cooper personally hired his teachers, a task other superintendents commonly delegated to subordinates. In this regard, he acted as a quality control check on personnel, but by so doing he was clearly declining to become a "scientific manager." Cooper's persistence in hiring and leading teachers was based on a small-town, nineteenth-century model. This placed him at odds with his peers nationwide, most of whom delegated such tasks as would the corporate chief executive officers they tried to emulate.

Teaching in Seattle was a desirable job, attracting young people with teaching experience from all over the country and keeping them for long careers. Teachers were the front lines of a system that promoted values of obedience to superiors, hard work, and aspiration. Yet a teacher rarely owned a house, was prohibited from working during vacations, had to resign (if female) when married, had no power to defend against dismissal unrelated to competence as a teacher, and had no way collectively to bargain for higher salary. In short, teachers were dependent people, whose daily lives were circumscribed by board policies.

Based on a sample of teachers in 1910–1911, Seattle was a magnet school district, attracting single women from small towns in the Midwest (two-thirds), the east coast (one-sixth), and the Pacific Northwest (one-sixth).[2] Rarely were these teachers the products of Seattle

---

2. Demographic information on Seattle teachers, 1910–1911, comes from personnel files of a 10 percent random sample of teachers. For similar data, obtained from seventeen states, see Lotus Delta Coffman, *The Social Composition of the Teaching Popu-*

high schools. The women who came to Seattle had not married— they viewed teaching as a career, and they were looking for a good school system. For many, teaching was the ticket out of a small hometown to a booming city.

The women who came to Seattle to teach were part of a newly emerging profession. In preparation, over half had obtained the two-year Normal School degree, and one-fourth had obtained the four-year Bachelor of Arts. Only 9 percent had not gone beyond high school. These latter had been hired before 1907–1908, when the minimum schooling for new teachers had been established as a Normal School education or its two-year equivalent. Since only veteran teachers were to be considered, Seattle could choose from a pool of experienced and successful women who knew they wanted to teach.

The women teachers were not young when hired. Half were between ages 26 and 30 years when first hired in Seattle, and one-fourth were between 30 and 40. The average age at hiring was 28.6 years. Those women who stayed the first few years tended to remain for long teaching careers. One-third of the grammar school women quit within six years. But one-third taught for more than twenty-seven years, with about 10 percent teaching for over forty years. Since all had taught elsewhere before Seattle, their time as teachers was actually longer. By age 65, three-fourths of those on the payroll in 1910–1911 had retired.

Almost all the grade school teachers were women, and they were unmarried women. Like most other cities, Seattle had a board policy against employing married women as regular teachers (although they could substitute, be school nurses and librarians, and, after 1912–1913, teach night school). Married women were perceived as having divided loyalties—first to husband and family, and then to teaching. Women who had prepared themselves to teach, who were successful teachers, and who wished to teach as a career, were forced to choose between marriage and career. The Seattle school

---

lation (New York: Teachers College, Columbia University, 1911). See also Cubberley, *The Portland Survey*, p. 55. The Seattle teachers, by comparison, are well-educated and experienced.

system was built by hundreds of women who chose to have a career.[3]

Most of the men teachers and administrators were also unmarried, had come from out of state, and were living in rented housing. Of these few men, those in grade schools were either waiting for a principalship or were manual training teachers (who did not stay long because they could make more money as tradesmen). Men waiting for a principalship may have waited longer in Seattle than in other cities. Cooper made it a point to hire a comparatively large number of women grade school principals.[4]

Despite the board's ongoing desire to hire more men, few men were added because of teaching's low salary and lack of status for men. Those men who stayed tended to be high school teachers and held university degrees. High school teachers were organized into their own group, separate from the Grade Teachers' Club, and they were paid more money. This salary "differential" was supposed to reflect the higher cost of university preparation. Cooper noted:

> In competition with other businesses in which men engage, teaching does not attract the number of highly qualified men that it would were the pay better, the tenure more secure, the chances of advancement more numerous, and the estimation in which the business is publicly held of more robust quality. The only chance

3. "Should any female teacher marry, her place shall become vacant at the end of the term" (*Rules and Regulations*, Board of Directors, Seattle Public Schools, 1902, section 19, article 7, page 11). The Seattle policy against employing married women was rescinded in 1947. As an example of how many women chose to remain as teachers, in 1920–1921, 401 of the grade teachers taught 5 years or less, while 678 taught 6 years or more (with 479 of those teaching 10 years or more). *Report of the Survey of the Executive Staff and Supervisory Staff of the Seattle Public Schools*, June 28, 1921, SP, Folder "Tax Reduction Council."

4. In his first year, Cooper chose a recent Stanford University graduate, Adelaide Pollock, to be principal of Queen Anne School. See Margaret Gribskov, "Adelaide Pollock and the Founding of NCAWE," in Patricia Schmuck, ed., *Women Educators: Employees of Schools in Western Countries* (New York: SUNY Press, 1987). Cooper subsequently appointed other women as principals, vice-principals, supervisors, and assistant superintendent (Almina George). In 1914–1915, 14 of 69 principals (20 percent) were women. In Cooper's final year, 1921–1922, 21 of 81 principals (26 percent) were women. For data, see "Comparison of Men and Women Principals, 1914–1934," SP, Folder "School Statistics."

which I can see of making the business of teaching more inviting is to make the pay sufficient to compensate for its apparent disadvantages.[5]

Board President William Pigott proposed in 1912 to establish a retirement system as a way to attract and hold men. Pigott, an industrialist who knew well about labor relations, admitted that "it is generally understood and conceded that the wages, tenure and age limit are not such, at the present time, to make the teachers' calling, especially for men, the desirable one it ought to be." Cooper acknowledged that about four times as many women as men applied for jobs in 1910–1911, so the women hired were superb teachers. To increase the number of men hired, "no male candidate of acceptable rating is denied."[6]

A national sample of teachers in 1910 gives some data against which to compare the above demographic profile of Seattle teachers.[7] Teachers in other cities tended to be about the same age as in Seattle. The median age for women in urban schools was twenty-seven years, and thirty-four for men. The median age when both sexes started teaching in urban schools was twenty years, significantly younger than the Seattle sample.

Seattle clearly attracted experienced teachers. The median amount of training for urban teachers nationwide was two years beyond high school for men and one year for women, both significantly less than that of Seattle teachers, where half of the women had a Normal School degree and one-fourth had a college degree. Cooper had set the standard, and he had enough applicants to hire only those with degrees. Seattle teachers were not only better educated and more experienced than their urban counterparts, but, like urban teachers everywhere, were significantly older, better educated, and more career-oriented than were rural or small-town teachers. Seattle teachers were part of an emerging career-oriented occupation that was struggling to achieve status as a profession.

5. Minutes of Board, January 31, 1912; ibid., March 8, 1915 (hire male teachers); *Annual Report*, 1910–1911, p. 32.
6. *Annual Report*, 1911–1912, p. 6; ibid., 1910–1911, p. 32.
7. See Coffman, *The Social Composition of the Teaching Population*, pp. 21, 25, 32.

An understanding was shared by teachers and the public about who teachers were and how they were to act. Although Seattle teachers were ranked near the top nationally in pay, they nevertheless were poorly paid. And they had an exceedingly high image to maintain. They were on public display, unlike anonymous workers in the big city. Each year a directory was printed with the names, addresses, and telephone numbers of the faculty. Teachers were to be properly dressed. They were to live in respectable apartments or boarding houses. They were not to drink or smoke in public, or give any hint of immorality.

When some aspect of the teacher image was tarnished, the principal, superintendent, or board stepped in. The board apparently had the legal right to dismiss people whose character did not fit the teacher image. Attorney H. W. Pennock reminded the board of its power "to employ and for cause to dismiss teachers," and that "no person shall be granted a certificate to teach in the public schools whose moral character or habits are known by the board to be bad." When complaints were filed against two male high school teachers, Board President William Pigott talked with them and they were put on probation. On several occasions the board instructed Cooper to chat with a teacher who had a delinquent bill.[8]

Cooper paid attention to teacher morale. He understood that good school systems hired capable teachers, then funded facilities and warded off constant indignities, thereby making it possible for faculty to teach well. Cooper saw his role as protector of and advocate for teachers, not only against outsiders but also occasionally against other administrators or the board.

A small incident involving teachers at Van Asselt School demonstrated Cooper's understanding of his role and his awareness that good teacher morale improved the quality of teaching. On behalf of the Van Asselt teachers, Cooper asked the board for carfare so they could take the Interurban and avoid the long walk from the end of the regular streetcar line. The board refused and instead directed that the pathway and sidewalks be repaired, with the cost not to ex-

8. Minutes of Board, February 24, 1922 (Pennock); ibid., June 12, 1912 (probation); ibid., April 28, 1915; ibid., October 18, 1918 (delinquent bill).

50

ceed five dollars.[9] This was an irritation to teachers who had to walk a considerable distance through rain, cold, darkness, and mud. For a minor amount of money, the Van Asselt teachers could have been treated better, just as other teachers in similar situations could have been helped. Cooper understood that a teacher who arrived wet and muddy started the day with a bad attitude and felt less than supportive toward her employer.

Teaching in a school system was normally characterized by prescribed curricula over which the teachers had little effective control. Textbooks were on a board-approved list and the subjects to be covered were established by the administration. But in the classrooms, the teachers worked alone, without another adult watching. Teachers made decisions constantly about what they really would teach. They emphasized some projects and chapters, hurried through others, rewarded certain behaviors, and looked the other way at some actions. Although the guidelines for what to teach, the consensus about how to teach, and the ethos of teacher conduct and the classroom value systems were all, in theory, decided for the teacher—in practice, the teacher could implement or sabotage the desires of administrators.

In Seattle, Cooper gave representatives of teachers an important voice in determining district curricula. Cooper worked with twenty committees of teachers and principals, preferring this slow process to a curriculum "made in the Superintendent's office and promulgated immediately by edict." Cooper preferred to give time for criticism and change in a plan. Teachers "best understand the problems involved," so should have a say in curricular change. Also, Cooper knew good ideas could surface through committee discussions, because "nearly all the leading city school systems and training schools of the United States are represented here by teachers who, before coming into this corps, had won recognition for work of superior quality according to the standard of the places from which they came."[10] Involving teachers not only produced better results, but promoted teacher morale.

9. Ibid., September 9, 1914.
10. *Annual Report*, 1910–1911, pp. 20–21.

Classroom procedures and detailed instructions for projects came regularly from the supervisory staff to the teachers, especially to grade school teachers. The few supervisors were subject specialists (e.g., drawing, music, manual training, penmanship). They gave workshops to teachers on how best to teach their specific subjects, and they spent time in the schools, observing and encouraging, to ensure that the subjects were taught correctly.

Two examples suggest the nature of supervisory direction. A 1908 three-page guide on "The Use and Care of Blackboards" made it clear that a Seattle teacher was not to use the blackboard in just any manner.[11] Some material was suitable to be kept displayed for weeks, and its location on the board was defined. Daily work was to be placed on the board before or after school. Material written during the day was for a lesson and was to be written by the students. Such detailed instructions presupposed that administrators knew the most effective ways to teach, and that all teachers should follow their guidelines. Such guidelines also helped create a sense of "the Seattle way" among the teachers, most of whom were new to the district.

A second example, a directive to second-grade teachers for a manual arts clay-modeling project, typified the instructions sent out by supervisors for special projects.[12] The memorandum stated when to do the project and how much time to take, instructed the janitor how to prepare and deliver the clay to the teacher, and told the teacher how to distribute the clay to pupils and how to clean up. Eight lessons were suggested briefly. These instructions helped to organize the logistics of the project, but left room for teacher alteration.

What might look like standardization and centralized control could also be seen as support from the central office to help break the bookish routine of the day. These instructions told the teacher how to reduce preparation and cleanup time, encouraging her instead to walk around giving help to students. Supervisors were con-

11. "The Use and Care of Blackboards," 1908, SP.
12. Clara Reynolds, "Instructions to First and Second Grade Teachers," April 20, 1908, SP.

Ross School, student garden plots, 1905. School gardening was very popular in grade schools. High schools had greenhouses for botany classes. (*Washington State Historical Society*)

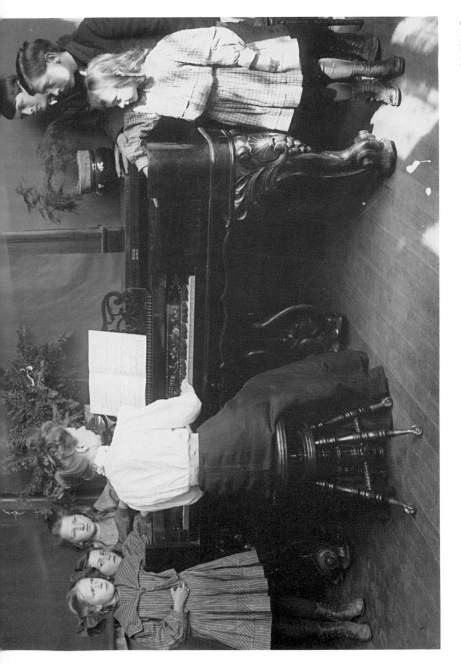

Deaf students feeling piano vibrations, 1909. Various special education classes were offered prior to World War I. (*Washington State Historical Society*)

High school life drawing class, 1905. Drawing was a basic part of the grade and high school curriculum. (*Washington State Historical Society*)

Lincoln High School, orchestra, 1914. Instrumental music was offered in high schools, including during evening school. (*Seattle Public School Archives*)

B. F. Day School, calisthenics, n.d. Physical education had become part of the grade school curriculum by World War I. (*Seattle Public School Archives*)

Queen Anne High School, girls' gym, 1913. (*Washington State Historical Society*)

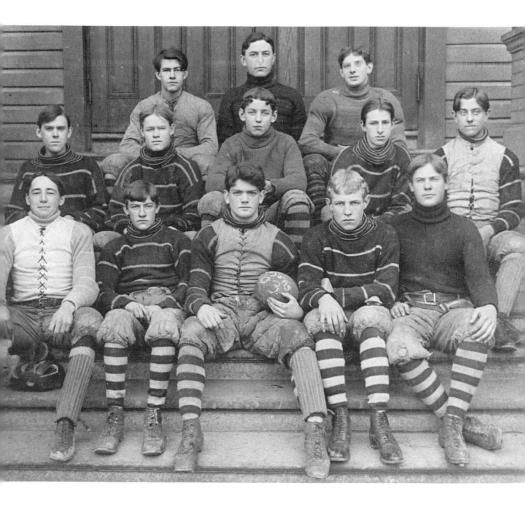

Ballard High School, football club, 1903. Club sports were organized and funded by the private Public School Athletic League. After 1910 interscholastic sports became part of the district's extracurriculum. (*Seattle Public School Archives*)

Franklin High School, boys' soccer, 1920s. Soccer was played during high school gym class, and at the grade school level. (*Seattle Public School Archives*)

cerned with promoting good teaching, not with record-keeping or room maintenance.

Continuing education for teachers occurred through the in-service teacher-institute days organized by the Seattle curriculum supervisors. Beginning in 1907, Seattle held a two-day teacher institute just before school opened in the fall. This was followed by three Saturday sessions in October, January, and March. "The daily routine of the school room tends to quench the fires of enthusiasm," wrote Cooper in support of teacher institutes. "Teaching is essentially a spiritual process," he thought, and these "fires of enthusiasm" need to be "rekindled from time to time."[13]

At these in-service planning days, teachers met with curriculum supervisors and principals to reinforce their sense of "the Seattle way" of teaching. These days were used to promote the curriculum, to demonstrate new teaching methods, to present new materials, and to improve teaching skills. For good reason, continuing education for Seattle teachers was presented in-house, during the school year, and was allotted five days. These teacher workshop days were intended by Cooper to help develop a sense of identification with the school district among the teachers, so many of whom were new to Seattle. Teaching methods were also discussed throughout the year at faculty meetings with supervisors and were reinforced by consensus among principals and teachers.

By knowing the detailed regulations and expectations of the Seattle system, teachers had an insider's knowledge of curriculum and pedagogy and, consequently, could not be replaced by just any well-educated person who also got along with children. Specialized knowledge of curriculum and pedagogy were necessary in order for teaching even to be considered as an emerging profession. For example, in 1907 the McMannis system of penmanship was adopted for the district. Years later, a supervisor of penmanship still saw to it that teachers correctly taught handwriting in this one approved manner. Knowing how to teach handwriting correctly, and actually teaching that way, made the teacher an expert authority.

13. *Seattle School Bulletin*, November 1915, pp. 2, 3.

Principals played an active role in the kinds and quality of teaching in their buildings. There were rules and procedures for teachers to follow, and the principal had to make sure teachers did things the way curriculum supervisors wanted. Principals also evaluated their teachers. The form was perfunctory, with principals rating teachers on a scale of one through four in general categories: knowledge of subject matter; industry; professional spirit; adaptability; success in teaching; success in managing; manner; influence; and comity. Many principals continued their professional education, taking classes, visiting schools in other cities, participating in study groups, and even conducting research and publishing articles.

Teacher's in-service institutes, curriculum guides, detailed instructions for lessons, evaluations by principals, visits from supervisors, and required after-school and Saturday classes with supervisors—all characterized centrally controlled and standardized schooling. But more important, all comprised the first steps toward making teaching into a profession. Teaching was emerging as a career that attracted educated people, especially women. In cities like Seattle, teaching was well-respected, white-collar, quasi-professional work.

Salary was the paramount issue among Seattle teachers in their drive for professionalism during the Cooper decades. Teachers regularly asked for raises, but they got what the board felt like giving—usually a curt turndown. When high school teachers asked for a raise in 1901, the board concluded that a raise would be "inexpedient," a word often used in subsequent years.[14] The board usually had enough money for a raise, but although it was willing to spend for bricks and mortar, it was reluctant to raise salaries.

Both the marriage rule and the salary structure of the Seattle school system discouraged teaching as a career. An assumption in the district's fiscal planning was that each year a considerable number of low-salaried women would resign (usually to marry) and be replaced by other low-salaried unmarried women. Women who stayed found that the salary schedule did not encourage long careers. The separate salary schedules for grade and high school

14. Minutes of Board, January 12, 1901; ibid., February 7, 1901.

teachers were based on years of service. The schedule was divided into five categories, and a teacher was advanced to the next step when a year was completed satisfactorily. In Seattle, veteran teachers led the drive to increase the number of salary steps beyond five, obtain an overall raise in salary, and create a retirement plan.

The difference between the grade and high school salary schedules was established in 1907. The board reasoned that because it had cost about $3,000 more for a four-year than a two-year degree, a high school teacher should get a 10 percent annual return on that expense. Cooper was adamant that this $300 differential reflected only the cost of college preparation: "I do not believe high school work is more difficult or more taxing than grade work, nor do I believe it is better done."[15] Nor did the pay differential exist because more men than women taught high school.

In the fall of 1908 the board created a problem by viewing salary steps as the way to reward a few outstanding teachers. They started a merit-pay system of sorts by giving sixteen grade and three high school teachers a double advance on the salary schedule. Such schemes were common nationally, but fell into disfavor by 1920. Most career teachers wanted an increase in the number of steps on the salary schedule, thereby making experience—not merit—the basis of salary increases.[16] The Seattle teachers had no formal way of taking a position on such an issue. Instead, they let Cooper speak for them, and on the issue of merit pay, he opposed even a limited merit-pay plan.

In 1911 and 1913 the board chose not to fund any meritorious teachers, citing a need for economy. The board then asked Cooper to reevaluate merit pay and tell them whether it was worth the money and effort. Cooper replied in January 1915, acknowledging his inability to "propose a merit system that would work out advantageously to the schools." Although he admitted that "there ought to be some way of properly recognizing degrees of merit," Cooper felt that merit pay created serious problems among faculty. The dif-

15. *Annual Report*, 1911–1912, p. 36.
16. See Wayne Urban, *Why Teachers Organized* (Detroit: Wayne State University Press, 1982).

ficulty was that "some of the best of school results are intangible and do not subject themselves readily to measurement." Those who felt they should have been rewarded, but were not, "lost confidence in the fairness of the management." Cooper cited reports of a merit-pay plan in another district which "does not increase the efficiency of the best teachers, and makes for unrest and dissatisfaction among those who . . . fall short of the best rating." If a successful merit plan could be created, said Cooper, it would require formation of a department to promote and evaluate "teaching efficiency."[17] The board made no changes, and a limited merit-pay plan persisted until after World War I.

Like any other employees, teachers occasionally needed time off during the teaching year, yet the board was slow to make provision for sick leaves or for extended leaves of absence. From 1906, teachers had twenty days of sick leave each year at half pay, but there were no provisions for extended illness. The teachers formed the Seattle Teachers Association in May 1911 in response to Cooper's request that they give financial help to those colleagues experiencing extended illness. About three-fourths of the faculty paid dues, from which sick teachers were paid $10 per week. The association also raised funds by sponsoring lectures and entertainments. The Seattle Teachers Association had a limited, well-defined purpose—it was a teachers' self-insurance group for long-term illness. It was not an advocacy group for teachers. In November 1912 grade teachers formed the Grade Teachers' Club, their main advocacy group.[18] Faculty were divided into groups along grade and subject lines, with Cooper as their spokesman to the board on issues of salary and welfare.

With the superintendent as their spokesman, with a mutual-aid society, and with several teacher groups organized along grade or subject lines, the Seattle teachers made no effort to organize a de

17. Frank Cooper, Memorandum to School Board, January 30, 1915, SP.
18. In the *Annual Report*, 1915–1916, p. 136, Cooper described the Grade Teachers' Club: "The organization strives to promote sociability among its members; to raise the intellectual and professional standard; to guard personal interests; to improve working conditions; to procure desirable legislation on all school questions; to be an instrument for good in the community."

facto union, unlike teachers in some other cities.[19] Fragmented into interest groups, Seattle teachers had no umbrella group under which to debate their issues or to take action. Cooper hired them, paid attention to their concerns, and acted as their spokesman before the board. Until the economic dislocation during and after World War I, Seattle teachers willingly allowed Cooper to be their advocate rather than their adversary.

Frank Cooper's primary concerns as superintendent were hiring the teachers, and then being their leader. He guided what they taught and how they taught, and he represented them to the school board. He saw himself as the "principal teacher," the leader of the faculty. Such a role had been workable when he was superintendent in the small town of LeMars, Iowa. It had worked even during his first years in Seattle. But as the Seattle schools physically outgrew the model of face-to-face administration, and as hierarchical and bureaucratic models from the corporate world became popular in other urban school systems, something had to change in Seattle. The Seattle schools physically outgrew Cooper's administrative style, and he knew it. With size came the beginnings of bureaucratic administration.

19. For history of teacher organization, see Urban, *Why Teachers Organized*; Edgar B. Wesley, *NEA—The First Hundred Years: The Building of the Teaching Profession* (New York: Harper & Row, 1957); William Eaton, *The American Federation of Teachers, 1916–1961: A History of the Movement* (Carbondale and Edwardsville: Southern Illinois University Press, 1975); and Robert L. Reid, ed., *Battleground: The Autobiography of Margaret A. Haley* (Urbana: University of Illinois Press, 1982).

4

Administrative Control: The Roots of Bureaucracy, 1911–1914

In 1910 an efficiency engineer named Frederick W. Taylor caught the nation's attention with some proposals for "scientific management" of business and industry. Taylor proposed analyzing a job, determining the most efficient way to do it, then seeing that workers did their jobs according to these procedures. This scientific management was designed to improve productivity in business and industry.

Historian Raymond E. Callahan has shown how Frederick Taylor's ideas spread rapidly to nonindustrial situations, including schools, where exaggerated claims were made for their usefulness. Taylor "was an outstanding, creative engineer, as well as a fine scientist," says Callahan, but when educational administrators attempted to bring his system into the schools, "they showed no real interest in, or ability to carry out, such painstaking research." Educators, vulnerable to mounting criticism that schools were run inefficiently, in 1911 and 1912 scrambled to adopt "Taylorism" and become businesslike. School administrators "were brought under even stronger criticism and were forced to demonstrate first, last, and always that they were operating the schools efficiently." In such a context, Callahan concludes, the superintendent was often transformed "from an educator to a business manager."[1]

Taylorism had only a modest impact on the Seattle schools. Ten years after Cooper had arrived in Seattle the school board continued to run the greatly expanded district in ways essentially unchanged

1. Raymond E. Callahan, *Education and the Cult of Efficiency* (Chicago: University of Chicago Press, 1962), pp. 18, 41, 47. See also Tyack and Hansot, *Managers of Virtue.*

from 1901–1902. Reuben Jones, hired in 1902 as board secretary, remained in charge of the business department: accounting, purchasing, and building maintenance. Jones had an assistant, a bookkeeper, a stenographer, and a typist. For years Jones was "the bureaucracy," hardly an organizational model from school efficiency advocates. Indeed, the manner in which Jones and Cooper divided administration (business and instruction), plus their longevity in their jobs, may explain why Seattle was slow to develop into a bureaucratically organized school system. The other central office employees consisted of a gardener, attendance officer, mechanic, and parental school superintendent. James Stephen, hired in 1903 as architect, employed a staff of draftsmen and construction inspectors. All these people reported directly to the board, rather than to Cooper.

The metaphors used by the board and Cooper to describe themselves were not those of the corporate world or of scientific management. In 1910 Cooper likened the schools to homes—"A school is a projection of homes. . . . Its ideals are representative of true home ideals. Its conditions and methods of management should approach as nearly as practicable to the highest type of home conditions and methods."[2] In keeping administration small, subservient to the board, and personal, the board and Cooper were bucking national trends.

The Seattle board's cautious approach toward enlarging the administration can be seen in its reluctance to add a second assistant superintendent in the spring of 1911. Instead, it directed Cooper to obtain statistics on the number of administrators in other similarly sized districts. Because the Seattle administration was smaller than others, it hired Edward Quigley as the new second assistant superintendent. That same summer, it also put H. W. Pennock on retainer as its lawyer. The next summer, it added Almina George as the third assistant superintendent. She became the highest ranking woman in the Seattle schools.[3]

Cautiously adding two assistant superintendents was hardly

2. *Annual Report*, 1909–1910, p. 36.
3. Minutes of Board, May 8, 1911; ibid., August 14, 1911; ibid., July 28, 1911; ibid., July 19, 1912.

Taylorism. The board's coolness toward the efficiency movement can also be seen in its November 1911 decision to remove all telephones from schools, because it thought telephone rates had been raised too high. For the next few years, communication between the central office and the buildings was by postcard or courier. In 1911, an organization whose leaders chose to have employees communicate by mail rather than telephone could not be accused of succumbing to "efficiency mania."

The efficiency mania in education peaked nationally in the summer and fall of 1912. In Seattle, the board still did little more than flirt with efficiency. It directed Cooper to prepare a table on each grade, showing the amount of time spent on each subject by each child, per day and per week. The board also wanted a chart showing the per pupil cost for manual training, domestic science, music, and drawing, and expenditures for the parental school. It also began a paperwork system, a sign that the district had grown to the point where limited records made for sloppy functioning. A job description of each administrator was drafted, complete with lines of authority. All central office people started to fill out time slips. And in February 1913, "all supervisors were directed to report monthly to the Board as to the use of their time by days."[4]

The most significant escalation of the efficiency perspective in the Seattle system came in August 1914, when the board hired William McAdam as chief accountant. One of McAdam's duties was to collect statistics showing efficiency in various departments and "GENERALLY: to these ends, to make a study of school finance and school method, so as to furnish the Board with all data which will enable them to determine the efficiency of every department."[5] This remarkable and powerful mandate was given not to the superintendent, but to an accountant under the direction of the board secretary, Reuben Jones. In Cooper's view, McAdam's hiring signaled the passing of "the period of contentment with opinion as a determinant of method or procedure." Although the use of statistics in

4. For national picture, see Callahan, *Education and the Cult of Efficiency*, p. 54. Minutes of Board, July 25, 1912 (per pupil cost); ibid., December 29, 1911 (time slips); ibid., February 5, 1913 (supervisor's report).

5. Minutes of Board, August 26, 1914; *Annual Report*, 1913–1914, p. 44.

decision making was not part of Cooper's background or spirit, it was an important part of the progressive era mentality.

Many professors of educational administration touted efficiency measures, and many superintendents embraced these techniques, whether from conviction or simply to preserve their jobs. Ellwood Cubberley, Stanford University's influential professor of education, promoted the educational efficiency movement in his widely used textbook *Public School Administration.* "The significance of this new movement is large," wrote Cubberley, "for it means nothing less than the ultimate changing of school administration from guesswork to scientific accuracy."[6] Efficiency did not mean running schools cheaply. Cubberley made it clear that good, efficient schools would cost plenty. They would, however, bring greater results than under-financed, poorly run schools.

Nationally, few prominent educators resisted the intrusion of efficiency strategies into school administration. Superintendents commonly implemented such techniques to better control their districts and, not incidentally, to attain a measure of prestige and to appease critics. Raymond E. Callahan has characterized those few who did dissent as "unavailing," because "in the total picture the dissenters were such a small minority that their voices were barely audible, and they were unable to stem the tide."[7]

Frank Cooper was not totally comfortable with "efficiency measures," and his name should be added to those who were "unable to stem the tide." Accountant McAdam and Superintendent Cooper occasionally sparred. For example, because there was a deficit in the free and reduced-price milk program, McAdam questioned its continued need. Cooper had made the decision on educational grounds (i.e., children too poor to get milk regularly need milk to develop physically and to perform well in school; therefore, the school is the place to dispense milk to everyone). The accountant questioned the decision on fiscal grounds (i.e., the program runs a deficit). The program's future was determined by the attorney on legal grounds

6. Ellwood Cubberley, *Public School Administration: A Statement of the Fundamental Principles Underlying the Organization and Administration of Public Education* (Boston: Houghton Mifflin Co., 1916), pp. 325–26.

7. Callahan, *Education and the Cult of Efficiency,* pp. 120–22.

(i.e., does the district have the legal authority to spend public money to subsidize the distribution of milk?). The program continued, but so did questions of that sort. Cooper's annual reports, following national trends, became much more detailed after 1914–1915, featuring such information as per capita costs, minutes per week on tasks, and the ages of students correlated to their rates of progress.

Cooper was not managing a large school system by looking at the charts, the "bottom line," or theoretical models. He was running the big city schools the way he had run the LeMars, Iowa, schools. Decisions were not made impersonally; there was no bureaucracy to hide behind, and a management-labor adversarial relationship hardly seemed plausible. Cooper's regular bulletins to principals reveal his detailed knowledge of buildings, curriculum, supplies, methods, and—judging from the advice he gave—the day-to-day problems. Cooper retained face-to-face, small-town ways in a booming city. He could do that because Seattle had a sizeable number of people who were building small-town neighborhoods with the local grade school at the center.

While Cooper was establishing himself in Seattle as an effective superintendent, he was also being noticed nationally. He was in close touch with his peers throughout America, as were they with him. Cooper annually attended meetings of the National Education Association (NEA) and was elected president of its Department of Superintendence in 1907. Regarding his annual trips to NEA conventions, Cooper told the board: "Our extreme location makes us, in a way, insular and prevents direct contact with the currents of progression and inspiration. . . . I may say that no influence has been so potent in keeping your superintendent alive and keen professionally as the effect of these meetings and the contacts they afford."[8]

Cooper knew what other school systems were doing, and he in turn was well-known and respected by others. But his reputation was not that of a technician. He was not, for example, part of the

8. Frank Cooper, Memorandum to School Board, January 3, 1917, SP, Folder "High Schools."

"Cleveland Conference," nineteen prominent educators identified with the scientific study of education. Nevertheless in the winter of 1914, having clearly not embraced Taylorism in his administrative style, Cooper was offered the superintendency of the Chicago public schools.[9] Cooper steadfastly remained a superintendent who was a "principal teacher." In the midst of Taylorism and administrative models from the corporate world, he proved that a superintendent could uphold the primacy of good teaching and still be recognized by his peers as a successful administrator.

Cooper believed firmly that the act of teaching well was to be supported and protected—not thwarted—by building and central office administrators. Even as the system outgrew face-to-face contact, and as efficiency schemes sprouted, Cooper measured every change by its impact on the classroom teacher. Teachers needed to be protected from principals who would feel free to interrupt a class with a telephone call (so Cooper opposed installing interschool telephones), or from efficiency-conscious administrators reorganizing the school day along industrial lines. Many of Cooper's superintendent colleagues would not have agreed.

By the time William McAdam was hired in August 1914, the district had increased its central office employees considerably over those few working when Cooper began. Yet it was hardly a bureaucracy when compared with most urban school systems. As superintendent, Cooper was not the chief executive officer presiding over incipient bureaucrats. Rather, a handful of people reported directly to the board (i.e., superintendent, board secretary, architect, construction inspector, mechanic, attendance officer, parental school superintendent, and gardener) and tried to manage parts of the burgeoning district. The Seattle administrative structure was not a textbook case of efficiency mania or educational bureaucracy.

Early in Cooper's second decade, the board could no longer supervise all details and listen to all reports from its administrators. Cooper told the board it had "connected itself directly with too many departments of work, to each of which it gives immediate at-

---

9. Tyack and Hansot, *Managers of Virtue*, p. 119; *Seattle Times*, December 3, 1914, p. 4 (Chicago superintendency offer).

tention and care. This is cumbrous, unremunerative, and withal unnecessary." Board members should not spend their time on "executive function." Besides, by dealing immediately with employees, the board was "giving opportunity for shifting responsibility and for friction." The solution Cooper advocated, citing Cubberley's *Public School Administration*, was for the board to centralize authority and deal with only himself and a business manager.[10] The board, however, did not attempt to reorganize the school administration until after World War I.

In the fall of 1913 the Seattle economy turned sour, prompting calls for "retrenchment" in public spending. In the previous few years, the city's bonded indebtedness had risen sharply.[11] Throughout 1913, vice as the major political issue was being replaced by middle-class fears about the economy and about political radicalism. Labor, Socialists, and the Industrial Workers of the World (IWW, or "Wobblies") were restive. Coal miners went on strike in Renton, teamsters struck in Seattle, and the shingle weavers (organized by the IWW) struck the cedar mills in Ballard. Through it all, the Seattle Employers Association tried to break labor and make Seattle an open-shop city.

Seattle's economic slump was reflected in school politics. Although voters annually approved excess bonds requested by the board, in 1913 a committee from the Tax Payers League requested that the board reduce expenditures. Despite a sizeable "no" vote, the excess bonds were approved. The board had a cash surplus of $200,000, but, reflecting the mood of the voters, decided neither to raise teacher salaries nor to build swimming pools at Ballard and Lincoln High Schools.

The economic slump also affected the 1913 school board election. Three incumbents ran for reelection—William Pigott, George Spencer, and Nathan Eckstein. Eckstein, a German immigrant,

10. Frank Cooper, Memorandum to School Board, December 30, 1916, SP. This memorandum quotes a passage on organization of school administration from Cubberley's *Public School Administration*.

11. Seattle's bonded indebtedness in March 1912 was $12,744,380, as cited in Clarence Bagley, *A History of Seattle from the Earliest Settlement to the Present Time* (Chicago: S. J. Clarke Publishing Co., 1916), p. 557.

had married into the Schwabacher brothers' wholesale grocery business. The Schwabacher company was part of the open-shop movement that sought to break the teamsters in their six-month battle with the Seattle Draymen's Association, the employers' group. Eckstein was a prominent civic leader, an activist in the Jewish community, and a frequent spokesman for businessmen. In a crowded field, labor did not run a candidate but wanted Eckstein defeated. The three incumbents, however, won easily.

The open shop remained the dominant political issue in the Pacific Northwest throughout 1914. The strikes of 1913, some violence in the teamsters' strike, the seasonally unemployed men who came to the cities each winter, and the depressed economy all led to some political realignment on the issue of labor. By the November 1914 general election, things were not going well for labor. The State Federation of Labor put an initiative on the November ballot to legislate an eight-hour day for the timber industry. Labor also worked against passage of an antisaloon initiative. The voters turned down labor on both counts. Historian Norman Clark notes that, after this defeat, union men were "inclined to jeer at political action as a cruel pipe dream, and the younger men were urging 'direct action'—the slowdown, the boycott, the strike." State Federation of Labor President Ernest Marsh had attempted to use the political tools of the progressives—reason, compromise, cooperation, universal suffrage, initiative, direct legislation—and had been rejected. "Cooperation and compromise," observes Clark, "were words that no one in the timber industry could use with a straight face in 1914."[12]

In December 1914 Socialist board member Richard Winsor ran for reelection. Nothing catastrophic had happened to the schools or to the district's credit rating during his first term, so the *Seattle Times* gave him its "unqualified endorsement."[13] Despite the fact

---

12. Norman H. Clark, *Washington: A Bicentennial History* (New York: W. W. Norton & Co., 1976), p. 113; idem, *Mill Town: A Social History of Everett, Washington, from its Earliest Beginnings on the Shores of Puget Sound to the Tragic and Infamous Event Known as the Everett Massacre* (Seattle: University of Washington Press, 1970), p. 155.

13. *Seattle Times*, December 3, 1914, p. 4.

that Winsor was seventy-eight years old and his health was sometimes a problem, he was reelected with the highest vote total to
date of any board member—4,914 votes.

The preamble to the 1914 Socialist platform of Richard Winsor
and Etta Tripp is instructive for its stated belief in public schooling
as a shaper of good citizens. This preamble would also have been
supported by union candidates:

> An ignorant people can never be a free people. Free education is
> the root and foundation of American democracy. Every lover of
> democratic institutions is therefore aware that the maintenance
> and protection of the public school is the most vital concern of the
> American people.
>
> The public schools serve as the colleges and universities of the
> great mass of the working people. Whatever makes for the im-
> provement and efficiency of the public school system is to the ad-
> vantage of the working class and good citizenship. The Socialist
> party, in behalf of public enlightenment and intellectual freedom,
> therefore champions the cause of the public schools, and is ever
> vigilant and zealous for their maintenance.[14]

This preamble expressed the moderate democratic-Socialism and
the conservative trade-unionism evident in prewar Seattle. A preamble written by radical Socialists and Wobblies would have delivered a stinging rebuke of the schools. The mainstream Socialists and
union men, however, wanted control of the schools, believing that
schooling made a difference in the chances of success for their children. They hoped to make schools even more accessible to working
people, more democratic in their control, and with a curriculum
more sympathetic to working-class concerns. The Socialists, for example, were strong advocates of kindergartens. After the legislature
had allowed free public kindergartens in 1911, Richard Winsor
pushed the board to open at least three new kindergartens each
year. And Winsor was always interested in the "proper deport-
ment" of students, fretting about "rowdyism and a disregard for the

14. Ibid., December 4, 1914, p. 3.

rights of others."[15] Socialists and labor advocated an expensive public institution, but the institution was clearly important to them.

Moderate Socialist and labor supporters envisioned the positive impact of schooling on citizenship and the future of the democracy. But the kind of paternal school system supported by Socialist board member Richard Winsor would soon be of little interest to the growing number of radicals among labor and the Socialists. It remained, however, of great interest to the vast majority of Seattleites.

15. *Laws of Washington*, 1911, 382, chap. 82, March 13; Minutes of Board, April 8, 1912 (kindergartens); *Annual Report*, 1913–1914, pp. 11–12 (Winsor).

5

Control and Morality: The School as Parent, 1912–1916

In the 1911–1912 *Annual Report*, School Board President William Pigott cited a theme that would become prominent in Frank Cooper's second decade as superintendent—the school as surrogate parent, interested in controlling all aspects of a student's physical and moral well-being. Cooper often described schools as extensions of ideal homes, with school employees playing a positive parental role. Pigott was more direct, claiming that "every move of the School organization is to uplift, and every act of the average parent and the existing social conditions is to tear down." He concluded that, for the schools to "hold out against this avalanche of demoralizing influences," the organization had to hire men and women "of the highest type" to be these surrogate parents, and to "redouble its energies . . . in every department of school life."[1]

Redoubling its energies came to mean involving the school in areas of a student's life previously reserved for parents—perhaps shared with the church, but certainly not with the public school. Between 1911–1912 and the American involvement in World War I, the school board, the superintendent, principals, and teachers all acted toward students with an increased sense of a parental role. Certain expectations for student health, morality, citizenship, and civility were now taught and enforced. These progressive educators were interested in controlling or influencing almost all aspects of a student's life, including things well outside the formal curriculum, such as neighborhood safety, interscholastic athletics, social dancing, sexual behavior, smoking, and secret fraternities. For students who

1. *Annual Report*, 1911–1912, p. 7.

were hungry, dirty, ill, delinquent, or dependent, the schools offered a variety of child welfare services, including a medical clinic and two parental schools for total custodial care of wayward youths. Cooper called the school "the state's chief child welfare agency,"[2] and indeed no aspect of a child's welfare seemed beyond school interest.

The Seattle school board's parental interest in its children and adolescents was similar to that expressed nationally by school boards, private and public child welfare agencies, juvenile court systems, and social workers.[3] One aspect of progressive era reform was an unprecedented interest in the welfare of the child by those outside the child's immediate family. For efficiency-minded as well as humanitarian progressives, education was the hope for the future. Hence, not only were all children and adolescents to be in school, but they were to be healthy, fed, and civil. The existence of large numbers of children who were sick, hungry, and uncivil had social consequences. Therefore, the situation needed to be rectified.

At some level in either the public or private sector, child-welfare advocates created new agencies to act as surrogate parents. This progressive era interest in child welfare went well beyond where public obligations had traditionally intersected with private family rights. Sometimes it evolved into meddling, where it took the form of institutional arrogance about the right and efficacy of agencies to improve the life-chances of children and adolescents. The record for

2. Frank Cooper, Memorandum to Board, January 14, 1921, SP, Folder "Clinic."

3. On progressive era interest in child welfare, see W. Norton Grubb and Marvin Lazerson, *Broken Promises: How Americans Fail Their Children* (New York: Basic Books, 1982); Ernest B. Hoag and Lewis M. Terman, *Health Work in the Schools* (Boston: Houghton Mifflin Co., 1914); Joseph Kett, *Rites of Passage: Adolescence in America, 1790 to the Present* (New York: Basic Books, 1977); Roy Lubove, *The Professional Altruist: The Emergence of Social Work as a Career, 1880–1930* (Cambridge, Mass.: Harvard University Press, 1965); David Nasaw, *Children of the City: At Work and at Play* (New York: Oxford University Press, 1985); Anthony Platt, *The Child Savers: The Invention of Delinquency* (Chicago: University of Chicago Press, 1977); Tyack, *The One Best System*; Peter L. Tyor and Leland V. Bell, *Caring for the Retarded in America: A History* (Westport, Conn.: Greenwood Press, 1984); Nancy P. Weiss, "Save the Children: A History of the Children's Bureau, 1903–1918" (Ph.D. diss., University of California at Los Angeles, 1974).

the Seattle schools, like most progressive era districts, was mainly of genuine help mixed in with some arrogant meddling.

The Seattle board took an interest in a student's welfare from the moment the student began the walk to school. It did not want students walking through physically unsafe areas or loitering near morally questionable businesses. Hence, it acted aggressively to keep the business community near a school free of undesirable elements. The board's objections to certain businesses ranged from their being "smelly" to being a "rendezvous of undesirable characters." Some of the businesses against which the board protested were: a horse stable, a candy stand, a hotel presumably used by prostitutes, an asphalt plant, a shooting gallery, an undertaking establishment, a moving-picture theater, an auto garage, a dance hall, and a skating rink. The board also used its influence to ban certain activities near schools, including slot machines, pool halls, and the distribution of advertising on sidewalks.[4] The board wanted these businesses and activities moved because it perceived schools as clean, wholesome institutions and itself as a watchdog.

As evidenced by repeated board concern with the same issues, not all students appreciated the board's attempts to protect them from their neighborhoods. Despite what reformers thought children should avoid on their walks home, most students no doubt knew the location of places to spend their pocket change or to loiter. The school board's occasional efforts at sanitizing school neighborhoods had more to do with an image for adults than with the reality of where some students spent their time or money.[5]

4. Various complaints by the school board against activities near schools are cited in following board minutes: March 28, 1906; July 11, 1904; July 7, 1909; August 13, 1909; May 24, 1911; January 23, 1912; February 10, 1903; February 23, 1909; and November 27, 1912. See also Frank Cooper, Memorandum to School Board, May 26, 1919, SP, Folder "Objectionable Buildings."

5. David Nasaw, in *Children of the City*, describes progressive era urban children who lived and worked in crowded neighborhoods. His findings, therefore, apply to a smaller number of children in Seattle than in most major cities. He notes (p. ii): "They were connoisseurs of the streets, devotees of the corner candy shops, the nickelodeons, penny arcades, amusement parks, vaudeville halls, cheap eateries, red-hot stands, and pushcart vendors. The money they earned magically transported them from the realm of dependent childhood to the world of consumption where money,

The board also protected the independence of its schools from people trying to sell products or services, promote a cause, or raise funds for charity. To stay independent, the prewar board chose to deny access to schools to all outsiders. School time was for classroom work, and no outside group, no matter how worthy the cause, was to take time away from students and teachers. The board's rule read: "Teachers shall not give notice of entertainments not connected with the schools; nor permit any of their time to be occupied by book or business agents, lecturers or exhibition men; nor allow a subscription or contribution to be solicted or taken up in the school for any purpose."[6] Fundamentally the board did not want its educators to share the schools' time with people over whom it had no control. The board guarded jealously the time for instruction and the control of the curriculum.

Once the students got to school, they often received some moral instruction. Following John Dewey, Frank Cooper believed that moral instruction went on throughout the day and could not be separated from other parts of the curriculum. Moral instruction was neither a formal subject nor a religious education. Dewey derided traditional moral instruction as "too goody-goody." He would have agreed with Cooper, who wrote that "the most effective moral instruction is that which is introduced incidentally, which comes at the psychological moment and which is accompanied at the time by an emotional element necessarily lacking when the discussion is introduced more formally and therefore appeals more largely to the intellectual side of the pupils." Cooper thought the staff was doing a good job of "giving pupils right motives for good conduct." He cited the lack of misconduct among pupils while walking to and

---

not age, brought with it fun and freedom." Nasaw concludes (p. 196): "The children grew up understanding far better than their parents the place of entertainment in twentieth-century urban life. A good time—at the movies, at the amusement park, or shopping in the dime or department store and wearing your new finery—was more than the reward for work: it was the reason one worked."

6. *Rules and Regulations*, Board of Directors, Seattle Public Schools, 1908, section 16, article 8, p. 16. The board denied school access to such groups as the Red Cross, Anti-Tuberculosis League, Elks Club, Salvation Army, YMCA, and YWCA.

from school, and the lack of evidence of vandalism on school buildings and furniture or in the toilet rooms.[7]

The Washington *Code of Public Instruction* mandated that teachers "endeavor to impress on the minds of their pupils the principles of morality, truth, justice, temperance, humanity and patriotism; [and] to teach them to avoid idleness, profanity and falsehood." To see how this was being done, Cooper in 1914–1915 solicited and received around eight hundred responses from teachers and principals. Teachers reported that they drew lessons from textbooks, the daily routine of the school, daily incidents, current events, celebrations of special days, memory work, picture study, and songs.[8]

The schools also tried to promote a wholesome, egalitarian environment through forming new character-building clubs and organizations. A federation of high school girls' clubs was formed in 1912. Girls' clubs gave school parties, put on programs, did volunteer work in hospitals, and encouraged interest in careers for girls. Cooper said the clubs were formed "to substitute the democratic spirit for the sorority, to help the lonely girls, to spread the influence of the stronger and better girls, to give girls wholesome but interesting good times, to place more girls in positions of leadership where executive qualities might be developed, and to set right standards in natural and unobtrusive ways."[9]

To promote the work of girls' clubs, and to help adolescent girls see alternatives to early marriage or low-skill, dead-end jobs, a girls' dean was hired in 1913–1914 at Broadway High School. Soon each high school had a girls' dean, whose duties included:

> Home employment for girls.
>
> The special supervision of girls without families or where the families are broken up.
>
> The oversight of girls here at school whose homes are outside of Seattle.

7. John Dewey, *Moral Principles in Education* (Boston: Houghton Mifflin Co., 1909), p. 43; *Annual Report*, 1914–1915, p. 50.

8. *Code of Public Instruction*, 1919, chapter 4, article 7, section 296, p. 96; *Annual Report*, 1914–1915, p. 49; Frank Cooper, Memorandum to School Board, May 11, 1914, SP, Folder "Moral Training."

9. *Annual Report*, 1912–1913, p. 58.

The advising of girls preparing for college.

Questions of dress and conduct and the physical life.

The planning of girls' work for girls.

The raising and expenditure of a fund to assist self-supporting
girls.

Vocational guidance.

The arranging of talks on topics of special interest to girls.

The encouragement of a wholesome social life for the girls.

Cooper liked having girls' clubs and a girls' dean, noting that "certain ill-advised movements starting among [the girls] may be diverted or stopped."[10]

Progressive era educators wanted to control or influence more of a student's life than educators had ever tried to do. A constant theme coupled distrust of what students would do when unsupervised by educators with confidence that the schools' formal curriculum and extracurriculum could make a positive difference. In addition to girls' clubs, the schools created an extracurriculum so they could control what students were already doing, and could thereby teach informally through activities. Two examples of character-building activities added to the extracurriculum were school sports and dances. But school involvement in these was not inevitable, nor was it widely applauded.

School involvement in athletics was a good indicator of the changing understanding of schooling from that of a strictly academic endeavor to something involving nonacademic aspects of a youth's life. Since 1904 the private Seattle Public Schools Athletic League, Inc., had financed, organized, and controlled an athletic program for grade and high school students. The school district had minimal involvement in this league. Teachers were to teach, not to ensure that the school team won and that students behaved while watching. This was exemplified in the *Seattle Times* editorial support of teachers at Seattle High School who had handed out "yellow slips" for low scholarship to some football players before a big game with Tacoma.

10. Nellie Buckley, Memorandum to Frank Cooper, February 5, 1915, SP; Frank Cooper, Memorandum to School Board, May 5, 1915, SP.

Athletics are merely a feature of the High School's playgrounds, not the important thing to be learned in the school. . . . The issuance of a few "yellow slips" a few days in advance of an important game shows that the faculty desired to deliberately impress it upon the players' minds that scholarship and not athletics is the principal thing in the High School work. The faculty would have been open to severe criticism had it done otherwise.[11]

By 1915 that attitude was superseded among educators, who now actively promoted and controlled an extracurriculum as a healthy part of the school's life. Cooper said the earlier attitude that "ignored" or "squelched" the extracurriculum was wrong, and was "as futile as to let them run without supervision was stupid. Both led to disruption of good school discipline." Henceforward, the sports to be played, the lessons learned, and the formal requirements for participation (e.g., physical examinations, parental waiver of legal liability) were to become important. Interscholastic athletics was to be the business of the schools. It was to be educative and tied to a sense of identification with a particular school. Cooper observed that the football team, "which was often a thorn in the school principal's flesh," had now become, "under proper management and advisorship," an outlet for "superfluous energies" and a way to develop "regard for law and order."[12]

Competitive sports were organized on a club basis by schools. Modeled after the New York Public Schools Athletic League, the Seattle league offered competition in football, track, and baseball. It was administered and funded by private citizens, with one representative of the school system on its board of trustees. High school sports were also organized on a club basis, funded by the participants and spectator fees, with football revenue covering the deficit created by the other sports.

Interscholastic sports were not directly controlled by the district, but the board kept a discreet eye on the program and sometimes moved to influence it. For example, in 1908 the board limited long

11. Thomas Cole, Memorandum to School Board, October 19, 1923, SP, Folder "Physical Education, 1914–1924"; *Seattle Times*, December 3, 1905, p. 6.
12. *Annual Report*, 1915–1916, pp. 116–17.

trips for athletics, and in 1910 it restricted play against teams outside the metropolitan area. Such contests, wrote Cooper, "introduce a professional element into high school games, or at least give them a professional flavor. The result in any case is not beneficial, but lends to high school athletic contests unneeded and demoralizing glamour of which there is now excess."[13]

In 1909–1910 the board moved toward taking control of interscholastic athletics. Such a transition from informal club sports to school-controlled extracurricular sports—with an educational purpose—occurred in most cities in the decade before World War I. In Seattle, the board began paying the salary of the athletic league director and put principals on the league's board. It also began paying the high school coaches and began searching for a high school athletic field.

In 1912, as the board was about to purchase an athletic field, an incident occurred which jeopardized not only that purchase but the board's new, tentative support of an athletic program. The incident that gave the board pause was a streetcar ruckus between boys from Broadway and West Seattle High Schools returning from a football game. The board condemned the incident, suspended all athletics, held up the $1,000 appropriated for athletics, and deferred a decision on buying a field. Four days later, student leaders from the high schools condemned the incident and blamed it on nonstudents. The board then reinstated athletics, "urging that their conduct be free from any cause for criticism in the future."[14]

The incident suggests that running an athletic program was opposed by some board members, and that going back to club sports not controlled by the board was clearly a possibility. District-supported sports meant expense and liability. More important, the right lessons and behavior had to be taught and learned. In 1913 Cooper

---

13. Ibid., 1909–1910, p. 35.

14. For national picture, see Timothy O'Hanlon, "Interscholastic Athletics, 1900–1940: Shaping Citizens for Unequal Roles in the Modern Industrial State," *Educational Theory* 30, no. 2 (Spring 1980): 89–103. See *Seattle School Bulletin*, April 1916, p. 4 (description of athletic program); Minutes of Board, October 20, 1909 (paid salary); ibid., October 7, 1912 (buying a field); ibid., October 11, 1912 (reinstating athletics).

proposed the following for coaches, underscoring his concern with sports as an educative activity:

> The Superintendent is authorized to suspend a coach at any time that it may appear that the coach fails to exercise proper discipline among or with members of any of the Athletic teams, permitting swearing, obscenity, smoking or similar offensive conduct, or unsportsmanlike conduct of any kind such as contentions or disputations with Umpire or other game officials, or who indulges in unsportsmanlike or other unbecoming conduct himself.[15]

Once the district took active control of athletics, it raised the inevitable question of which sports to play. To fit into an understanding of athletics as educative and wholesome, certain sports might not qualify. Football was specifically at issue because of the high incidence of injury and the high risk of serious injury. Most grade schools dropped football in favor of soccer. Indeed, in 1914 one grade school principal persuaded his students to drop league football and instead use that money for what became a successful, yearlong intramural program for both boys and girls.

In mid-November 1916 a player was seriously injured in a Broadway versus Lincoln High School football game. The board directed all high school principals, "in view of the serious accidents that have occurred, to report on the advisability of substituting soccer for football in the schools." The board discussed the football game in which the boy was hurt, and the school medical inspector, Ira C. Brown, M.D., expressed concern "pertaining to the alleged use of stimulants by football players" and the "alleged overplaying at the games."[16] Football continued as a boys' high school sport, along with basketball, baseball, track, and tennis. High school girls played in-

---

15. Minutes of Board, June 19, 1913.

16. *Annual Report,* 1914–1915, p. 82 (intramural); Minutes of Board, November 22, 1916 (soccer for football); ibid., December 4, 1916 (Dr. Brown). Dr. Brown had earlier expressed concern about overexertion in sports. In 1914–1915 he had tried to ban all foot races beyond 100 yards: "I know of nothing except it be eight oar boat racing that requires such expenditure of heart muscle as in these running races" (*Annual Report,* 1914–1915, p. 111).

tramural basketball, baseball, and tennis. Grade school students competed in soccer, baseball, volleyball, handball, and track.

Cooper actively promoted in-school sports for adolescent girls. The girls, said Cooper, otherwise "stood around talking or watching the games of the boys, or talked, or engaged in aimless activity of no physical and questionable moral value." High school gymnasium teachers visited grade schools and successfully taught games and sports to the older girls. The schools also offered free swimming lessons at public beaches. These lessons were especially aimed at girls. The swimming teachers were to be women, because, noted Cooper, "boys generally need but little encouragement in learning to swim; girls much more."[17]

Educators had misgivings regarding the schools' involvement in interscholastic sports; the general public did not. The public wanted a strong, school-sponsored interscholastic sports program. Educators had fewer qualms, however, about another part of the extracurriculum—school-sponsored dances. They wanted to sponsor school dances so they could teach acceptable dancing styles and enforce proper student behavior. The public, however, was sharply divided over whether dancing was any business of the school. This issue provoked the most public concern, debate, and depth of feeling of any school issue before World War I.

In Seattle, dancing emerged as a symbol of how the new middle-class school supporters saw their schools. They wanted their neighborhood schools to look clean and neat, without unsupervised children loitering on the playgrounds. They wanted deviant, delinquent, and dependent youth shipped out of their neighborhoods and to the parental schools. They wanted their teachers virtuous, dedicated, and on a pedestal. And they did not want their schools turned into dance halls. In a city with a wide-open, sleazy side to it, the new neighborhood gentry certainly did not want their symbol of progress sullied by dances. That young people would dance was bound to happen, but elsewhere, not at school.

The new professional educators were worried about the negative

17. *Annual Report*, 1914–1915, p. 81 (sports for girls); ibid., 1915–1916, p. 126 (swimming lessons).

influence of private dances. They wanted, however, to create and control a school extracurriculum. They were confident that the best place to dance was at school, where they could teach and supervise acceptable behavior. Consequently, high schools were allowed two dances per year (Junior Prom and Senior Ball) under school sponsorship.[18] The board could have avoided controversy by stating that dancing was not the business of schools and ignoring what occurred at private dances and clubs. But educating the whole child meant influencing as much of the young person's environment as possible. Dancing, along with free milk, medical care, school sports, and parental schools, was all part of schooling's larger endeavor to shape literate, healthy, and moral citizens. The issue of dancing showed that parents were sharply divided on how to promote a positive moral climate. The district clearly could not speak for all.

School dances became a public issue when Principal V. K. Froula of Lincoln High School invited a dancing instructor to give a twenty-minute talk to students on modern dancing, "and to illustrate the acceptable steps and their execution." Froula did this just before the January Senior Ball, hoping to discourage the new style of "exaggerated and grotesque forms" of dancing. Froula was concerned about his role as principal when undesirable behavior occurred during school dances. He expained his dilemma to Cooper:

> The matter of the new style of dancing has been a source of the most serious annoyance to the High School principals. It has meant the personal interference of the principal with young people on the floor for one thing, a most unpleasant experience. . . . Boys of this age are supersensitive when they are out with their girl friends, and all their American independence combined with Medieval chivalry come to the surface under this provocation. . . . The High School principals felt that they could no longer hold out against

18. Regarding dances outside school control, see *Seattle School Bulletin*, November 1915, p. 3: "although passing as high school functions and popularly believed to be under the school management and guardianship, [dances] could not be properly controlled either as to the character of the guests or as to conduct. . . . It was made necessary for the board to choose between having these affairs outside and unregulated or having them in the school buildings and regulated."

the modern dance and therefore undertook to try to direct and guide it.[19]

Froula's attempt to encourage more modest dancing was viewed by critics as the school's teaching dancing. Two issues emerged in the protests to the board: (1) dancing leads to immorality; and (2) students who do not attend school dances are socially ostracized. In a letter to Cooper, a group of parents asked that school dances be ended. They disapproved because "we regard the necessarily familiar attitudes of opposite sexes in the dance, particularly at the high school age, as liable, quite frequently, to lead to baneful results." In addition to this moral argument, parents opposed dances because the children whose parents would not let them dance must "either go contrary to their parent's wishes, by dancing, or be ostracized to a pretty large extent from the social affairs of the school."[20]

Encouraged by the principals, the board reaffirmed that each high school could have two annual dances, and the grade schools could have folk dances. In June 1915, petitions against dancing came to the board, the lengthiest with 1,700 signatures from the Washington Public School Welfare League. The issue of dancing was debated again in the fall, and in early 1916 the dancing policy was again reaffirmed.

The concern over dancing was fundamentally a concern over sexual behavior, a topic the board reluctantly but dutifully dealt with when it had no other choice. Undoubtedly board members hoped that adolescent passion would not result in issues with which the board would have to deal. But it did, of course. Cases of "immorality" were reported to the board, and the offending students were often suspended. Married students were sent to different schools or were dropped. And sexually active adolescents were sent to the parental schools. The board did better with bricks and mortar than with its institutional response to sex. Perhaps the most curious example of efficiency-minded board members, who were not sure how

19. V. K. Froula, Memorandum to Frank Cooper, January 21, 1915, SP, Folder "High School."

20. Minutes of Board, January 20, 1915 (protest); Letter to Frank Cooper, February 24, 1915, SP, Folder "High School."

to deal institutionally with adolescent sex, can be seen in the two-year sex-segregation experiment at Broadway High school, 1914–1916.

Concern for efficiency in learning and with adolescent sex roles resulted in placing boys and girls in separate classrooms. Cooper was opposed to this experiment, as were the Federation of Women's Clubs, the Congress of Mothers, and Parent-Teacher Associations. Socialist board member Richard Winsor called it an "attempt to turn the wheels of time backward."[21] Nevertheless, an article in the October 1914 *Seattle School Bulletin* justified instruction segregated by sex for reasons of efficiency and psychological development. The *Bulletin* article argued that some psychologists believed that, because high school boys "differ in point of maturity and mental alertness from girls of the same age, it is better for them and also for the girls to be instructed separately, because neither responds or reacts in the same way." To promote efficiency, the article postulated that "different treatment for the sexes at this particular age is desirable in order to secure the best results from instruction." Therefore, to determine if instruction to students segregated by sex was better for the needs of the students and the school, Broadway High School was chosen for an experiment.

The data after the first year of sex segregation were hardly rigorously collected or analyzed. Of the fifty-three teachers affected, twenty-four favored segregation, seventeen were opposed, and twelve saw no beneficial results but were not strongly opposed. One teacher complained that "discipline is harder in the boys' classes. The boys are not so careful as to body posture and general courtesy when alone." Another teacher felt that girls were "deprived of the privilege of having any men teachers except in rare instances," as men were to teach boys. And one teacher commented that "girls' classes are too inert. I miss the energy contributed by the boys." Basically, the science teachers liked segregation because boys moved faster and did more advanced work. One teacher said, "I would say that boys have done 30 to 40% more work than in mixed classes."

21. *Annual Report*, 1909–1910, p. 36 (Cooper); Minutes of Board, April 9, 1913 (women's clubs); ibid., May 23, 1913 (PTA); *Annual Report*, 1912–1913, p. 11 (Winsor).

With girls, the teachers weakened the material. A teacher observed, "In physics, I have been able to leave out much of the most difficult part for the girls and to do more extensive work in the parts in which they are naturally most interested."[22]

Based on the data showing better achievement for boys, and with lukewarm faculty support, Principal Thomas Cole recommended that a modified form of the experiment continue for another year. Noting that "it would hardly be safe to draw any very definite conclusions after so short a trial," Cooper went along with the decision for a second year.[23] Much of the decision to continue sex segregation was based on the notion that girls were poor in mathematics and science. In the principal's view, boys were to study science and mathematics more seriously than were girls, and bright girls were not expected to be bright scientists or mathematicians. This experiment may not have created preconceptions about what boys and girls should study or become, but it certainly promoted and perpetuated stereotypes.

Not all adolescents were interested in the attempts by their schools to make them wholesome, moral, and civil. Some students smoked, drank, cheated, fought, were sexually active, and did not care about the school's agenda. References in board minutes to vandalism, locker theft, weekend rowdiness on playgrounds, and fights after football games all remind that some youth misbehaved. Such attitudes and behavior were an affront to the high moral and behavioral standards of the school. They were also a challenge to priggish educators, who now assumed the obligation of changing the ways of rebellious and delinquent youth.

The school employees most directly concerned with antischool youth were the attendance officers. Starting in 1904, the appropriately named Truman Ketchum was hired as attendance officer. Ketchum rode the streetcar or a district-issued motorcycle and tracked down truant youths, issued citations to negligent parents, granted work permits to youths under age fifteen, and pursued employers who hired underage youths. A 1909 state law gave attend-

22. Thomas Cole, Memorandum to Frank Cooper, May 7, 1915, SP.
23. *Annual Report*, 1914–1915, p. 51.

ance officers police powers, including powers of search and arrest. But the attendance officers also viewed themselves as social workers, acting as intermediaries between deviant, delinquent, and dependent youths on the one hand, and social service agencies or the juvenile court on the other. Cooper called truancy "an effect, not a cause," declaring it the business of the attendance officer "to find the cause back of the effect and to deal constructively with that cause."[24]

In February 1914 the district hired a female attendance officer called a "school matron," a position advocated by the Socialists. The matron worked with girls "showing tendencies toward delinquency." She made home visits and counseled parents and their daughters. Most referrals came to her from principals and dealt with attendance, sexual activity, and discipline. She referred cases to the juvenile court or parental school, and she also had the power to put girls on probation, to report weekly to her.

The board did not want students in school who would be bad influences. One example of this was board concern with boys illegally getting and smoking cigarettes. Section 5, Article 9, of the *Rules and Regulations* of the board prohibited smoking or the use of tobacco on or in the vicinity of the school grounds, with suspension and expulsion as punishment. The board interpreted this to include going to and from school. The board, central office administrators, and principals all actively worked to eliminate smoking among students. Cooper wrote that "the principals through various agencies such as talks to boys in assembly, in groups and as individuals, seek to show how the practice of smoking interferes with physical growth and good scholarship."[25]

Another example of the board's trying to eliminate outside influences within its schools was its several-year battle against secret fraternities. The board wanted an egalitarian school environment in which social and economic distinctions between students were minimized. Secret fraternities made a mockery of this goal. A fraternity had persisted in the high schools since 1901, so in 1905 the board

24. *Quinquennial Report*, 1916–1921, p. 62.
25. Frank Cooper, Memorandum to School Board, March 24, 1915, SP, Folder "High School."

proposed to deny fraternity members any school privileges, including a diploma. The issue went to court, and the board was upheld by the Washington Supreme Court. The court concluded that fraternities "foster a clannish spirit of insubordination, which results in much evil to the good order, harmony, discipline, and general welfare of the school." Nevertheless, references in following years to fraternities indicated that they persisted in secret.[26]

In 1914 Cooper began informing the board when school nurses and attendance officers reported incidents of "moral delinquency." The board directed that such students "be reported at once to the Superintendent, and that if in his judgment they should be prosecuted in any way, they be referred to the Attorney of our District, to take up with the proper officials of the courts."[27] School required certain standards in the personal life of students, and it removed those who flouted the expectations. If a child were morally delinquent, responsibility for dealing with the child still rested with the parents but was now also shared by the school authorities, including the superintendent and board.

Shared authority for morally delinquent youth was most fully expressed in the the boys' and girls' parental schools operated by the Seattle school district. These were residential schools where school-age youth who were headed for delinquency were sent to be reformed. They were not school-operated prisons for convicted juvenile delinquents. The school district as an agency of the state was understood to have the legal right to establish a residential school and to compel students to live there until paroled.[28] In practice, school authorities (e.g., principals and attendance officers) worked closely with the juvenile courts in determining who should be sent to the parental schools.

Why did the Seattle school system build isolated reform schools

---

26. Minutes of Board, May 7, 1901 (fraternity); "Report on Fraternities," undated, SP, Folder "Fraternities." Diplomas were to be denied to anyone who became a fraternity member after April 26, 1905. The court's decision in *Wayland* v. *Board of School Directors of Dist. No. 1* of Seattle is reprinted in *Pacific Reporter 86* (September 1906): 642, and in *School Review* 14, no. 10 (December 1906): 739–45. See also, *Annual Report, 1909–1919*, p. 34.

27. Minutes of Board, February 4, 1914.

28. *Laws of Washington*, 1903, 109, chapter 78, March 12.

on Lake Washington's Mercer Island and at Brighton Beach for total custodial care of wayward youth? Such institutions could have been owned and financed by city or county government, with the school district merely supplying teachers. Indeed, the state ran institutions for delinquent boys. That the schools took responsibility for total care of deviant and dependent children was in fact the logical extension of progressive era confidence in education. A totally controlled environment was an educator's ultimate test of the reforming powers of schooling.

The parental schools must have imposed a financial drain on the school district, but clearly the board felt a sense of duty. Board minutes over the years were filled with budgetary requests for the parental schools. The board almost never turned down these requests. Seattle juvenile authorities did not want these youths in their neighborhoods, but taxpayers did not want to pay too much to care for them. Rather than fund their custodial facilities through general government or the prison system, the Seattle public schools chose to fund facilities as best they could.

The boys were in grade school. Most were young adolescents, ages 12 to 14 years, but some were as young as 5 years. The average age in 1914 was 13.1 years when admitted, and 13.8 when paroled. By grade level, they were mostly behind.[29] The Mercer Island school had facilities for 100 boys but was always overcrowded. Parole, therefore, was generous.

The boys were sent to the parental school for various reasons, such as alcoholic parents or broken homes. In 1910–1911, of the 153 boys who were in the school at one time or another, 43 were judged to have had an intemperate father, 5 an intemperate mother, and 5 with both parents heavy drinkers. Only 39 had both parents living, 5 were orphans, 12 had only a father, 16 only a mother, and 21 lived with a step-parent. A 1917 list included the following reasons for sending boys to the parental school:

> Mother deserted family; father alcoholic; serious neglect.
> Incorrigible; indolent and slovenly in habits.
> Harmful companions; late hours; irregular school attendance.

29. *Annual Report of Parental School*, 1910–1911, p. 12.

Shiftless mother.

Father dead; mother has cancer; boy dependent.

Moral and physical neglect; father dead; malnutrition.

Bad sex habits.

Vicious disposition; immoral surroundings.[30]

The school board took charge of not only the boys' emotional, intellectual, and spiritual development, but their physical development as well. Boys were sent to the dentist, fitted for glasses, vaccinated, and operated on when necessary. After the school medical clinic opened in 1914, parental school boys were often sent there for medical and dental work. After treatment, they were immediately shipped back to Mercer Island because, admitted Parental School Superintendant Willis Rand, "the nurses have not the time and patience required to keep such lively patients in bed."[31]

The boys all worked in the cottages, kitchen, and laundry, and on the farm. Each boy had his own garden, and they all shared in the work of the orchard, the farm crops, and the animals. In manual training classes, they made items for use around the farm, and the older boys did some carpentry and building. All boys daily attended school. On Sundays they attended Sunday school run by visiting church people. The church and state distinction was blurred by the perceived value of religious education for the delinquent boys.

Parole was determined by a point system tied in part to the dinner table. Every time a boy broke a rule, he received a demerit. Each month the boys were grouped by their demerits and were fed better or worse accordingly. If a boy did not fight, swear, or smoke very much, or if he did not vandalize the property, engage in "immoral acts or conversation," lie, steal, or run away, and if he was also fairly obedient and courteous—then he could leave the school in four months. Few did. Most boys stayed about nine months.[32]

30. Frank Cooper, Memorandum to School Board, August 15, 1917, SP, Folder "Parental Schools, 1914–1923." Report to School Board, August 12, 1917, SP, Folder "Parental Schools."

31. *Annual Report of the Parental School*, 1910–1911, pp. 7–9; Willis Rand, *Annual Report*, 1914–1915, p. 112.

32. Frank Cooper, Memorandum to School Board, January 20, 1915, SP, Folder "Parental Schools."

When the boys were paroled, they reported monthly to the principal of the school they attended. The principal acted as a parole officer and could recommend that a boy be returned to the parental school. Perhaps the nine-months' average stay was long enough to make the boys want not to go back, but not so long that they became institutionalized. In 1910 Cooper claimed that "eighty-five percent are turning out well," but he also acknowledged that "the chief difficulty in making certain of good results is the lack of a favorable environment following the liberation of the boys."[33]

There were other local institutions for youth. The board felt an obligation to educate those adolescents also, even with no formal authority over the institutions and with only token obligation. For example, the board periodically supplied a teacher to the juvenile court's detention home; the Children's Orthopedic Hospital; the Everett Smith Home; the Crittenden Home Association; and the Ruth School for Girls.[34] The line between public and private social welfare groups was often blurred.

From 1904 until 1914 the district had no formal provision for delinquent or dependent girls. Requests for a girls' parental school were constant, coming from Superintendent Cooper, the school nurses, the Federation of Women's Clubs, and from some board members. In 1914 the district took over the Girls' Home and Training School, a home for thirty-five girls which had been started by club women, who had hoped the district would take responsibility. After running this school for five years, the board bought a larger site on Lake Washington and built a new girls' parental school. When that opened, the girls were isolated in a sparsely populated area of the city, but were not rusticated on an island farm like the boys.

As with the boys, reasons for which girls were sent to the parental school were based on assumptions about desirable family life and behavior, and on an observer's judgment about the degree to which that girl failed to meet the expectations. The girls were mostly ages

33. *Annual Report*, 1909–1910, p. 26.
34. Minutes of Board, February 21, 1912 (detention home); ibid., March 20, 1912, and June 5, 1912 (Children's Orthopedic Hospital); ibid., June 5, 1912 (Everett Smith); ibid., June 5, 1912, and January 22, 1913 (Crittenden); ibid., January 6, 1922 (Ruth School).

fourteen to sixteen, with some as young as ten. Representative reasons for sending girls to the parental school were comparable to those for boys:

> Sex experiences; harmful influence at school.
> Dependent child; moron; father alcoholic and sexual degenerate; same true of mother.
> Practices secret vices; disregard of property rights.
> Untruthful; hard to control.
> Sex experiences; parents separated; mother immoral.
> Unsanitary home; improper home environment; petty thieving; truancy.
> Parents dead; mother died of syphilis; both alcoholic; sisters delinquent.
> Mentally defective; morally irresponsible.
> Parents divorced; mother overindulgent; socially precocious; mother a waitress.[35]

The criteria for sending boys and girls to the parental schools would indicate that the board took actions it had a legal right to take. More important, given funding and a supportive political climate, the board felt it ought to take such actions to influence positively the health and welfare of needy minors. As noted, there were sometimes disagreements within the system over whether specific acts were any business of the schools, and there were also legal challenges to some board actions. But generally, before World War I, there was remarkable agreement among the board, Cooper, school-supporting citizens, and the legislature on the board's parental role as an agency of the state. The actions taken and the institutions built by the Seattle schools, and by other school districts nationally, were unprecedented in American school history.

Progressive era educators understood their mandate broadly— every child was entitled to schooling and social welfare services. Hence the district ran parental schools, supplied teachers for the

35. Frank Cooper, Memorandum to School Board, August 15, 1917, SP, Folder "Parental Schools, 1914–1923."

children's hospital, created special education classes, and hired auxiliary teachers to give small-group instruction. But progressive era educators also wanted to be efficient. To serve all children as efficiently as possible, educators devised and began to use intelligence and achievement tests. Such testing provided a diagnostic tool to determine the efficiency of pupil placement in special school programs, and it provided a check on teaching and learning rates.

Intelligence testing was developed in 1905–1908 by the French psychologist Alfred Binet to suggest which students were significantly advanced or retarded in their learning capabilities. Such tests were Americanized, notably by Stanford University's Louis M. Terman (1916), then were reworded by Robert Yerkes and colleagues for use among army recruits in World War I. Numerous standardized achievement tests were developed contemporaneously. For example, Edward Thorndike created widely used achievement tests for arithmetic (1908), handwriting (1910), spelling (1913), drawing (1913), reading (1914), and language ability (1916).

Seattle, unlike many other cities, used achievement and intelligence tests sparingly and cautiously during Cooper's tenure. Echoing Binet, Cooper cautioned that intelligence tests "are not held to be definite and accepted facts, but they are largely suggestive of conditions only. They have proven most helpful in pointing out possible defects or abilities possessed by the children, a knowledge of which has given to the teachers clues to successful methods of approach."[36]

The first achievement test given in Seattle (1913) was a sixth grade arithmetic test. Seattle students scored only about average. Consequently, the district began to reevaluate its arithmetic program and to expand its testing. It bought 3,000 copies of arithmetic and English tests developed by S. A. Courtis, director of research for the Detroit Public Schools. The Courtis tests were given in June and September 1913, with new expectations for their usefulness. Cooper explained that "educational practice, which has always rested for the most part upon personal opinion, is seeking a scientific basis." With these tests, "the problem of the teacher is thus more clearly de-

36. *Annual Report*, 1913–1914, p. 60.

fined. The need and kind of individual instruction required by pupils is indicated quite definitely." After the results came back, conferences were held with teachers, and Assistant Superintendent Frank E. Willard told them he "looked for improved results in the schools."[37]

Cooper discussed the results of the Courtis tests in his 1913–1914 *Annual Report*, noting for the first time how Seattle children compared with those of other cities. What these comparisons suggested to Cooper was that, because of individual differences, group instruction in arithmetic was unsatisfactory. Instruction would "have to be more personal."[38] The Courtis tests caused Cooper concern about the number of students scoring below average, and the apparent need to change methods. Standardized testing, with national norms for comparison, ended provincial certainties about doing an outstanding job.

The consequences of school districts comparing their achievement scores were significant. What material was taught, and how it was taught, was now tied to scores on examinations and was compared with other cities and with national norms. Individual teachers had to keep their students from consistently scoring below those of other teachers. Cooper noted that "a low score does not necessarily mean poor teaching. There may be reasons for it that are entirely legitimate, but they should be well known."[39] Superintendents had to keep their districts from scoring too low. Prestige and job tenure were now linked to this "diagnostic tool." Seattle, in 1914–1915, began to "teach to the test" by using practice materials developed by Courtis.

In 1913–1914 Cooper started to ask educational questions in terms he had not previously used. Testing and measurement, as well as the efficiency movement in school administration, had focused his awareness on individual differences rather than the group. "The class," he said, "is becoming more strictly a group of individuals." Later he reflected that "the teacher's greatest problem is to diagnose

37. Ibid., 1912–1913, p. 38 (Cooper); Minutes of Board, February 18, 1914 (Willard).
38. *Annual Report*, 1913–1914, p. 51.
39. Ibid., 1915–1916, p. 95.

the individual needs of her pupils and then so to adjust her work that she may be able to give each child the thing that he especially needs in the way that he needs it to promote his best growth."[40]

Many progressive era educators understood efficiency to mean a bureaucratic structure, scientific management (Taylorism), and a great interest in testing and measurement. Cooper and the Seattle board were not enthusiastic advocates of efficiency in these forms. The seeds of bureaucracy, Taylorism, and testing were blown into Seattle during the Cooper years. A few germinated, but Cooper did not tend them. They grew and bloomed in the 1920s.

After a decade as superintendent, Cooper could reflect on the success of the district. Seattle high schools were bulging with students, night schools were popular, the district had a remarkably high percentage of its youth in school, and there really was not a large urban underclass of adolescents to menace the social stability. Nevertheless, for progressives who were interested in retaining as many students as possible, a disquieting number of adolescents still dropped out of school.[41] Concern over adolescent school dropouts was national. In Seattle, this concern was reflected in a several-year study of dropouts.

In September 1913 the Seattle board asked Anna Y. Reed, a young Ph.D. (sociology, psychology) with an interest in vocational education, to gather data on school dropouts. Reed attempted to learn who dropped out of school, why they dropped out, what happened to them after leaving school, and what could be done in the future to prevent this inefficiency. For two years, Reed traced 402 grade school and 822 high school dropouts. Reed's 1915 report was not received enthusiastically by the board.[42]

40. Ibid., p. 70.

41. For dropout statistics, see George D. Strayer, *Age and Grade Census of Schools and Colleges: A Study of Retardation and Elimination* (Washington, D.C.: Government Printing Office, 1911).

42. After submitting her report, Reed heard nothing from the school board for two months ("either of appreciation or censure"), so she offered to resign, but did not. See Anna Y. Reed, Letter to Reuben Jones, April 20, 1915, SP, Folder "Vocational"; idem., *Seattle Children in School and Industry* (Seattle: Board of Directors, Seattle Public Schools, 1915); and idem, *Vocational Guidance Report, 1913–1916* (Seattle: Board of Directors, Seattle Public Schools, 1916).

Reed's major conclusion was that Seattle adolescents dropped out of school not because their families were poor and they had to work, but rather because they did not like school. Many dropped out on the verge of academic failure. Of those who went right to work, most were in dead-end jobs. Reed's conclusion that the dropouts found school irrelevant to their lives challenged the board's smugness. She found no external factors such as nationality, size of family, economic necessity, age, or a combination of such factors to explain dropouts. Quite simply, the curriculum did not seem worthwhile to the variety of adolescents who left school.

Standards within high schools were high. Crowded conditions created pressure to drop those who were failing so as to give that chair to someone else. Yet, Reed argued, it was inefficient to have people drop out and make false starts on several jobs, all without prior benefit of counseling and curricular options more closely tied to the world of work. Reed was genuinely concerned about adolescents who left school too early, who did not have marketable skills, and who consequently would have fewer job options in life. Cooper shared Reed's concerns. He lobbied the board to create programs connecting the school with the workplace, thereby improving the transition for students who left school early. "The schools have not been 'hitting the bulls eye,' " responded Cooper, "because they have been aiming at a big target having a not well defined center." It was time to follow up, to see "what and where we have hit," and to make some changes.[43]

As a result of Reed's reports (1915, 1916), the board established a Director of Vocational Guidance. Subsequently, a vocational division was created, encompassing attendance, evening schools, vocational guidance, part-time schools, and a job placement bureau. The vocational guidance department coordinated vocational advisers in each high school, and some assistants in grade schools. "Vocational guidance," declared Cooper, "is as much a responsibility of the public schools as moral, cultural, health and civic guidance."[44]

43. Frank Cooper, Memorandum to School Board, January 27, 1915, SP, Folder "Vocational."

44. The 1919 state legislature passed a law requiring four hours per week school attendance of all persons under age eighteen who were employed.

Anna Y. Reed's reports did not signal a strong new interest in school dropouts in Seattle. Rather, attention in Seattle remained focused on the steady increase in attendance, with Seattle always at or near the top nationally in the percentage of children and adolescents in school, and the length of time they stayed. Superintendent Cooper and the board offered classes for all ages, from kindergarten to adulthood, and many daily affirmed their high regard for schooling by attending some kind of class.

6

Efficiency and Health: The School Medical Department, 1914–1916

One hallmark of progressive era educators was efficiency. This was not just from a desire to imitate the corporate world's alliance with Frederick Taylor's scientific management. Rather, the educators' concern with efficiency came from their real problem of coping with large numbers of students flocking to new schools and staying through high school. Once a casual and informal endeavor, school was becoming a mass institution, requiring substantial amounts of tax money. The questions of what to teach, under what conditions, by whom, and to whom all had a new urgency. Seemingly innocuous queries—"How many desks need to be in each third grade room?"—necessitated answers in the form of specific, systemwide policies. Such policies would now define the curriculum, the length of the school day and year, promotion standards, class size, teacher certification, and the amount of money necessary to run the system.

Seattle school progressives coupled an interest in efficiency with a broad understanding of their role in promoting the intellectual, moral, and physical welfare of students. They tried to make an egalitarian ideal a practical reality—every child should attend school as long as possible and should learn enough to be self-sufficient and a good citizen. "Efficient" was not a synonym for "cheap." The district broadened the curriculum, hired auxiliary teachers for students needing help, added social workers and attendance officers for truants, and began a part-time school and night school—all as ways to give second chances to students who would otherwise drop out or be pushed out of school. Efficiency meant keeping each chair filled, but it also meant not consigning any youth to a perceived life of fail-

93

ure because that student's school experience had been a failure. Efficiency included a high regard for the eventual social price of school failure. Efficiency meant paying attention to details, so that almost all students were schooled—and then it meant worrying about those who were not.

Seattle's educators would also attend to the physical health of children. It was inefficient to have children ill, injured, or unaware of how to keep themselves healthy. Medical inspection of schools gained popularity in leading eastern cities after 1904–1905, and hiring a school district medical doctor became acceptable after 1909–1910.[1] In March 1914 the Seattle board hired Ira C. Brown, M.D., as its first medical inspector in charge of the newly reorganized school medical department. Thus began a remarkable period of involvement by the school system with the health of its students.

With Dr. Brown, a school clinic was built on one floor of the old administration building. He greatly expanded the medical and dental services, increased the number of nurses from two to twenty-four, looked after the health of teachers, and issued bulletins on everything from classroom temperature to playground safety. Dr. Brown also persuaded the board to buy him a new Studebaker at a time when curriculum supervisors, nurses, and attendance officers rode the bus.

Dr. Brown came the closest among Seattle school officials to the progressive era ideal of efficiency-minded school administrators. Such administrators were interested in bureaucratic structure, deference to expert authority, the use of statistics in policy making, and the avoidance of surprises. Brown was a former United States Army medical doctor who specialized in medical problems resulting from large numbers of men living in close quarters. He acted on school health questions in a manner commensurate with his military background. Brown's goal was to eliminate medical problems as the reason for poor student achievement. He maintained that "a child who does not keep up in his grade is a medical subject."[2] If inefficiency in

1. See Louis Rapeer, *School Health Administration* (New York: Teachers College, Columbia University, 1913), p. 76.
2. *Seattle School Bulletin*, December 1914, pp. 2–4.

schooling (i.e., falling behind one's grade) could be reduced by treating medical problems that contributed to the failure, then it followed that the school must treat such problems

Lewis M. Terman, who became a prolific writer and influential professor of education, wrote in a 1914 textbook on school health that it was "legitimate to levy upon the school for any contribution it is capable of making to human welfare." That radically new purpose for schooling was quickly to become the "conventional wisdom" among both humanitarian and efficiency-minded progressive educators. Terman, for example, hoped that through the school medical department, the society would be delivered "from a burden which is more oppressive than the burden of militarism; for physical inefficiency, sickness, and premature deaths are costing us as much as all our crime and as much as a good-sized perpetual war besides." Terman claimed that "not more than one-third of our school children are free from physical defects prejudicial to health."[3]

Seattle's medical effort was part of a national effort by child advocates to use the school as the agency to upgrade the health of children. Spurred by the United States Children's Bureau and the NEA annual conventions, and influenced by reports and books, the school health movement quickly gained adherents among urban educators. A 1913 national study of school health efforts concluded: "Compulsory education seems absolutely to involve compulsory health and the most economical way for a community to provide adequate diagnosis, prevention and continued or intermediate treatment is through the instrumentality of the public schools."[4]

Modernization required that someone in authority formally teach employees and students how to do things previously learned informally or not at all. The school medical effort provides a good example. In Dr. Brown's view, students who came to school dirty needed to be instructed on sanitation and given baths. All students needed to be taught in a physical education class how to exercise. Girls needed to be taught how to care for infants, and mothers how to

---

3. Lewis M. Terman, *The Hygiene of the School Child* (Boston: Houghton Mifflin Co., 1914), p. 11; ibid., p. 8.
4. Rapeer, *School Health Administration*, p. 229.

care for their older children. All children needed to be immunized. And temperatures in all school buildings had to be kept at a certain level.

Brown's military background influenced his ideal of an efficient school administrator. Plans were to be made for all possible contingencies, potential problems were to be systematically eliminated, and standards were to be set to which everyone must conform. The schools were to run smoothly and uniformly, without pupils being slowed by the irrational and unnecessary problems of sickness, epidemic, preventable accidents, lack of medical attention, or hunger.

As school medical inspector, Dr. Brown had four main areas of supervision: first, he supervised the school nurse program; second, he ran the school clinic; third, he inspected school buildings and grounds, looking for things that would adversely affect student health and safety; and fourth, he ventured into Cooper's territory—the curriculum.

Dr. Brown's chief administrative task was to supervise the school nurses. Seattle hired its first school nurses in 1908. These were public health nurses who concentrated on school children and their families. The nurses fought communicable diseases, screened students for health problems, made house calls, and taught health and hygiene. The presence of school nurses also reassured some middle-class parents that the schools actively promoted middle-class standards of cleanliness and health. Cooper claimed the nurses "helped to make the general average of personal cleanliness in the school rooms the same as that in the good homes of the community, so that the children from the best home environment need not fear contamination from school room association."[5] Additionally, the nurses were social workers and advocates for poor children.

5. Frank Cooper, Memorandum 35 to Principals, January 10, 1908, SP. Mrs. Edith M. Hickey and Miss Bertha Harris were the first Seattle school nurses, beginning in January 1908: see Minutes of Board, January 17, 1908. According to Hoag and Terman, *Health Work in the Schools*, pp. 48, 49, the first school district to hire nurses was New York City in 1903; in 1907, only eight cities had nurses—but by 1910, eighty cities. See also statistics on the work of nurses in *Annual Reports; Annual Report,* 1912–1913, pp. 54–55.

Dr. Brown's vision of the nurses' job came from his roles as public health crusader, military man, and efficiency-minded progressive. He saw the school as the logical agency to improve the health of children and their parents. Nurses were not hired to do first aid, but were to be nurse-educators, teaching students and their parents about the care of infants and children. For example, Brown told Cooper he wanted nurses to instruct the sixth through eighth grade girls in baby care in half-hour classes after school. He asserted:

> In this way we will reach many mothers of today and nearly all of tomorrow. . . . When it is recalled that more babies die from neglect because of the ignorance on the part of the mothers than do from disease contracted in the ordinary manner, it would not take long before this system would be felt in a practical way by reducing the great mortality among infants.[6]

The nurses were expected to share Dr. Brown's energy, commitment, and enthusiasm for improving the health of children and preventing contagious diseases. Brown and the six nurses worked Saturdays and year-around so that, according to Brown, "their whole time could be utilized in visiting homes and getting the children to the clinic, thus saving many school days that are lost during the school term."[7]

Nurses carried a staggering caseload. As itinerants, they rode the streetcars, making the rounds of schools, setting up shop wherever they could in a building, and visiting homes of students out with prolonged illness. They were paid ten dollars per month extra for carfare. They kept regular days and hours in buildings so that mothers could come to them with questions. The home visits were to "change intolerable conditions by patient instruction and demonstration, and thus [to] have a cleaner and better fed child in the class room." These nurses were tireless workers, meeting lines of children in one school after another. That nurses lived up to Dr.

---

6. Ira C. Brown, Memorandum to Frank Cooper, May 28, 1915, SP, Folder "Clinic."

7. Ibid., June 2, 1914, SP, Folder "Clinic."

Brown's high expectations is suggested by his compliment to them for working longer each day than eight to five, "more than half of the time and never a word of complaint."[8]

A major emphasis of the nurses was to prevent and combat communicable disease. Medical science had no effective way of treating such highly contagious and deadly diseases as smallpox or types of influenza. Hence, public health workers emphasized prevention. Nurses taught children and mothers about sanitation. Inspectors from the Board of Health inspected school toilets and plumbing, closed schools, and ordered children to stay home and off streets during an outbreak. Such tactics were not controversial. But without immunization, they also were not very effective. Consequently, vaccination as a condition for school attendance became an important issue.

Because vaccination affected all school children, an unvaccinated individual was seen as a menace to others. At issue was whether the state could compel children to attend school and be vaccinated as a condition of attendance. Conversely, could the state compel attendance and not compel vaccination, knowing full well that unvaccinated children were more likely to catch, carry, and spread an infectious disease for which there was no cure?

Vaccination as a condition of school attendance was first proposed by the Seattle Board of Health and was made school board policy in 1902. Compliance with this vaccination rule was less than total, and enforcement was lax. The periodic requests from the city or county suggest that vaccination of all school children was not really made a condition for attendance.[9]

8. In Dr. Brown's first year, 1914–1915, the six nurses gave 75,839 examinations (the school system had 37,000 students). The nurses also visited 5,984 homes, treated 3,803 cases of minor sickness or injury at school, reported 280 cases of contagious diseases, and took 216 throat cultures. See Ira C. Brown, "School Medical Inspection," in *Annual Report*, 1914–1915, pp. 107–08; idem, Memorandum to Frank Cooper, May 28, 1915 (home visits); *Annual Report*, 1913–1914, p. 78.

9. Minutes of Board, January 7, 1902. On November 7, 1903, the Seattle Board of Health asked the school district to see that all students were vaccinated. On September 8, 1908, the King County Medical Society recommended compulsory vaccination for school children. On October 30, 1908, the school board agreed to have the superintendent enforce the vaccination law, "and to provide free vaccination for all who are unable to pay for the same."

Parental objections to vaccination surfaced in 1908 when the Anti-Vaccination League asked the school board to suspend or modify the vaccination policy. The board challenged the league to test in court its vaccination policy, which was based on the Washington *Code of Public Instruction.* Two weeks later the superior court upheld the school code and ruled in favor of the board. The parents appealed and lost again.[10]

The milk program was another example of the involvement in student health by Dr. Brown and the nurses. Brown examined a number of children referred by the nurses and concluded: "It was not medicine but food that they needed. . . . They complained of lack of energy, sense of chilliness, and frequent colds. The remedy was plain to me to be milk, whole milk." Starting in 1915, he attempted to improve the health of "anemic and malnourished children" by using the school as the agency to distribute milk daily. Brown asserted that "fresh milk, being the most important, is therefore the most beneficial food that a child can have. There is no condition in the life of school children with which we have to do where milk is not desirable."[11]

Dr. Brown called the milk program successful, as schools were distributing about 5,000 bottles per day after four months, and "many of the children [were] already showing color in their cheeks and an increased activity." Students paid various amounts for milk or got it free, depending on their family income. Not to draw attention to poor children, students paid ahead of time by buying milk tickets. Brown noted that free milk could be a problem, as there was the "danger of training children to be paupers." Incipient pauperism aside, Brown supported the milk program, claiming "the sole object being to get to the poor children all the milk that they need whether it be for two cents or nothing."[12]

Dr. Brown and Cooper were also concerned about the eating hab-

10. Minutes of Board, November 13, 1908; *Code of Public Instruction,* article 3, section 254, no. 11, p. 82, 1919. *McFadden* v. *Shorrock,* 55 Wash. 209, established that the legislature has power to require all minors to attend the public schools and all pupils to be vaccinated.

11. *Annual Report,* 1915–1916, p. 127; *Seattle School Bulletin,* January 1916, p. 3.

12. *Seattle School Bulletin,* January 1916, p. 3; *Annual Report,* 1915–1916, p. 129.

its of students at lunchtime. Earlier, Cooper had advocated providing lunch in grade schools as an alternative to the "sweetmeats, doughnuts or pie" the children were bringing. Nothing was done until Brown arrived, repeating the same themes: "There are many children who eat no breakfast and at the noon hour purchase a handful of cheap candy." Two lunchrooms were started, with more following quickly, in both grade and high schools. The school was not to ignore poor nutritional habits, but was to teach the right lessons even at lunch.[13]

In addition to supervising school nurses, Dr. Brown presided over a large, well-equipped medical and dental clinic in the old administration building. The medical and dental services offered at the clinic had started informally as charity work. By 1910–1911 four physicians had volunteered their time on a regular basis to check referred students, and by 1914 these charitable services had evolved into a clinic. Nurses referred children whose parents could not afford a private doctor. The justification for running a school clinic was that children who needed medical attention, and who would otherwise not receive it, should be treated at school expense to increase their chances of staying in school, performing their best, and, it was hoped, improving their lives.

The school clinic was open every day and was staffed by volunteer physicians and partially paid dentists. The treatment was given at low cost or free, Dr. Brown declaring that "inability to contribute does not in any way change the final result. We take care of the child in any event." Eyes were examined, teeth filled, and minor surgery performed there so that children would not have to visit the city clinic at the police headquarters. Brown did not want children at the city clinic, because "little girls after the operation are put to bed next to a prostitute perhaps or some other unfortunate woman and on the men's side the boys are placed next to a drunken individual or a dime-novel hero and the effect is apt to be bad; besides in the vicinity of the Police Headquarters there is an atmosphere of positive harm for young minds." In 1916 the board hired Maybelle Park,

13. *Annual Report*, 1910–1911, p. 30; ibid., 1913–1914, p. 72.

M.D., as assistant medical inspector, responding to requests for a woman doctor for the girls.[14]

A third area of Dr. Brown's involvement was the inspection of buildings and grounds for health and safety reasons. Brown functioned as a self-appointed gadfly, poking into all aspects of school life and, in effect, asking why certain people had done their jobs incorrectly so that results now adversely affected the health of students. For example, Brown issued reports on ventilating problems in which he told the engineers, architects, and building inspector what they had done wrong. Brown even believed he should inspect classrooms and rearrange desks, so that "the occupants may receive every advantage from light effects."[15]

In addition to inspecting school buildings, Dr. Brown involved himself in checking playground safety. In 1915, worried about medical bills and liability lawsuits resulting from children injured anytime on school grounds, the board asked Brown and Assistant Superintendents Willard and Quigley to find ways to reduce playground accidents. They recommended removing just about all playground equipment, and the PTA, Congress of Mothers, and Play Leagues protested vigorously.[16] The issue had to do not only with injury and liability, but with the educators' desire to control and supervise play. To an emerging profession, play was to be educative. Misbehavior on playgrounds was miseducation. The educators

14. *Annual Report*, 1913–1914, p. 71 (treatment cost); Ira C. Brown, "Permanent Organization," undated, SP, Folder "Clinic" (city clinic); idem, Memorandum to Frank Cooper, June 6, 1916, SP, Folder "Clinic" (Dr. Park; girls' advisors). For more on the history of the school clinic, see *McGilvra* v. *Seattle School District No. 1*, 113 Wash., January 1921.

15. Ira C. Brown, Memorandum to School Board, March 8, 1915, SP, Folder "Building Improvements"; idem, Memorandum to Frank Cooper, November 19, 1914, SP, Folder "Building Improvements." See also *Annual Report*, 1913–1914, p. 77.

16. The report read: "A. The abandonment, as soon as practical, of all playground apparatus that in use takes children off the ground or floor, with the exception of the giant stride and the slide. B. The removal from the school premises of all horizontal bars, overhead ladders, vaulting poles, teeter boards, swinging bars, high swinging rings, and any other apparatus that offers similar opportunities for injury. C. That a substitute for the discarded apparatus be provided through a system of physical training along the lines indicated in detail by Superintendent Cooper in a report to the Board on Physical Training under date of September 20, 1915."

wanted their teachers to be in charge of play on school property, or not permit after-hours use of schoolgrounds. Educators had a high view of their role and a low view of the child when they were not around to supervise.

Dr. Brown was an aggressive, confident health activist who offered an opinion about or wanted to help supervise almost every aspect of school life. Consequently, in his fourth area of responsibility—curriculum—Brown entered Cooper's turf and caused some acrimonious disputes. For example, Brown proposed to remedy curvature of the spine in 15 percent of the students by having each teacher lead prescribed exercises "at the same hour and in the same manner throughout the system."[17] Cooper supported "free play" for grade school exercise, and he winced at Brown's ideal of all children doing the same exercise simultaneously throughout the city.

Dr. Brown saw his mission of health education as overwhelmingly important. His attitude was a direct challenge to Superintendent Cooper. For Brown to tangle with the superintendent over curriculum meant that Brown felt no need for a medical doctor like himself to be deferential to an educator. Brown was, in effect, castigating the regular curriculum for not teaching practical, everyday "life-skills," which he maintained were taught through his Little Mothers' League. For Brown, schools were not only to shape students into good citizens—literate, knowledgeable, thoughtful, and employable. Rather, Brown wanted to also teach a generation to stay physically healthy, so as not to become a societal burden.

Dr. Brown and Cooper also disagreed over the schools' role toward mentally retarded children and youth. Humanitarian progressives like Cooper thought mentally deficient children should attend special classes, designed to help them live as normal a life as was possible. Severely retarded children should go to a state institution. Efficiency-minded progressives like Brown thought the school should test and classify retarded children, treat some medically, and send the others home or to a state custodial institution. Brown considered it a waste of school resources to maintain classes for mentally deficient children whose future looked bleak. He thought the

17. *Annual Report*, 1913–1914, p. 76.

socially efficient thing to do was to see that these children did not reproduce. The board chose to listen to Cooper, and created special classes for different degrees of mentally retarded children.

Classes for retarded children were started in 1909–1910 at the Cascade Special School. The children were screened by volunteer doctors and by the psychological clinic at the University of Washington. This testing provided information to the teachers so that each child could have an individualized instructional program, "having in view the development of whatever motor and intellectual capacity the child may have." More children were judged to need special schooling than space allowed. In 1911–1912, 348 children were examined, and 125 were recommended for the Cascade Special School. But there was room to enroll only 65. In pushing for more classes, Cooper argued that "these children gain nothing by being associated with normal children. The regime of the ordinary school is in no way suited to their needs. Their instruction is necessarily individual and their learning must involve more motor activity than is permitted in schools for other children. They need more real things with which to work."[18]

Cooper hoped the individualized instruction would result in "the highest development possible for them," with some becoming self-supporting. Cooper acknowledged: "They will not be cured" through these classes, but "they will be lifted to better things and developed as far as possible." Nellie Goodhue, principal of the special school, intended to place each retarded child "in a school environment where he can be best developed to the limit of his capacities."[19] Only the most severely retarded were to be sent to the state institution at Medical Lake.

Cooper was pleased with the success of children in the Cascade Special School. He observed, "For the first time these handicapped children find themselves working with their equals. No longer is the slow pupil of the class subjected to the taunts and jeers of the other

---

18. Ibid., 1909–1910, p. 27 (testing); ibid., 1910–1911, p. 24 (Cooper).

19. Ibid., 1909–1910, p. 26, and ibid., 1910–1911, p. 24 (Cooper); ibid., 1911–1912, p. 30 (Cooper); Nellie Goodhue, Memorandum to Frank Cooper, May 9, 1918, SP, Folder "Special Schools."

children."[20] The Cascade School spawned the Child Study Laboratory, a more scientific setting housed with the school clinic. A child psychologist from the University of Washington and several specialist doctors worked closely with these children. Here they conducted an observation class to watch, evaluate, and learn about retarded children. The children were then recommended for a special class or were banned from school.

Both Dr. Brown and Cooper saw institutionalization as proper for severely retarded youth. Cooper believed those "clearly outside the field of public school education" should go to state institutions. Cooper suggested that school authorities "should have the right to procure the commitment of all children who cannot be developed mentally to an institution for the feeble minded for life." This would remove them from society, be in their best interest, and would keep them apart so they would not reproduce. District personnel actively tried to persuade parents of children judged severely retarded to apply to Medical Lake. Cooper concluded that "we work for the time when all such children, as well as society, may be protected by their proper institutional segregation."[21]

Dr. Brown was not convinced the expense and effort of the special classes was worthwhile. He thought it was "wrong to attempt and more so to practice making of such children partially self-supporting with a view of turning them loose upon the community or even under the supervision of some kind-hearted person who would work them much in the same manner as an animal." Brown saw as troublesome the prevalent humanitarian ideas exemplified by special classes for retarded children: "Added importance is attached to every life, more care is taken of the weak and sickly, the poor, the criminal, the lunatic and feeble minded, with a result that more survive to perpetuate and increase their numbers." He pronounced it "a waste of time and money to try to educate an imbecile or idiot." He believed rather that they should be institutionalized:

> Every mentally defective person is a potential criminal. We delude
> ourselves when we believe that by training the defective child's

20. *Annual Report*, 1911–1912, p. 30.
21. Ibid., 1911–1912, p. 30; ibid., 1911–1912, pp. 30–31; ibid., 1913–1914, p. 63.

hands we are educating him and thus adding to social security, an admitted result of education. Making a potential criminal self-supporting increases his dangerous possibilities. If this be true then safety lies in institutional care of all children in the idiot or imbecile class.[22]

Dr. Brown was frankly worried about the "constantly increasing number of mentally deficient children." Sharing a theme from the eugenics movement, he implied that the long-range solution was to prevent mentally deficient people from reproducing. "The only practical way of approaching this problem," he said, "is to have an educational campaign vigorously conducted until such time as it is safe for one to discuss freely the means of prevention." Since eugenic solutions were not discussed freely, institutionalization was the best alternative, to avoid "propagation of their species" and for "protecting society against their possible unlawful acts."[23]

Dr. Brown felt almost everything to be the business of his medical department, much to the chagrin of Superintendent Cooper. Brown proposed that he, rather than educator Nellie Goodhue, be in charge of all retarded children. Brown had no qualms about going ahead on a project that was in someone else's department, and then casually mentioning it later to the superintendent: "I was going to wait until sometime later to make an extended report upon this, but mention it now simply to show you what can be done in a corrective way with these children."[24]

Dr. Brown exasperated Cooper with his wide range of projects, not all of which had been authorized. As examples, Cooper was annoyed by Brown's attempt to cure speech problems with X-ray treatment; Brown's "wholly untenable recommendation of the principle that the ventilating outlet should be placed near the ceiling"; his Little Mothers' League ("not sound pedagogically"); his advocacy of a physical training class borrowed from the United States Army; his

22. Ira C. Brown, Memorandum to School Board, July 3, 1916, SP, Folder "Special Schools"; *Annual Report*, 1914–1915, p. 110 (waste).

23. Ira C. Brown, Memorandum to School Board, July 3, 1916.

24. Nellie Goodhue, Memorandum to Frank Cooper, May 9, 1918, SP; Ira C. Brown, Memorandum to Frank Cooper, May 16, 1918, SP.

proposal to the board that student promotions be dependent upon passing a physical examination ("wholly indefensible proposition"); and his attempt to take control of physical training in grade schools. Cooper noted: "If Dr. Brown would remember that he is by training and by experience a medical man and not an educational man and would seek light upon educational phases from educational sources just as an educational man would seek light upon medical phases from medical sources, he would avoid mistakes and difficulties."[25]

Progressive era educators differed significantly among themselves. Ira C. Brown and Frank Cooper represented two disparate types of progressives. Brown approached the organization of large numbers of people by wanting to be efficient—by which he meant prevention, preparation, and the use of statistics to help make policy. Cooper was not as concerned with quantified data, social efficiency, and getting the most for each dollar. Cooper was interested in providing teaching and learning conditions that would allow widely differing individuals to learn to their potential, with cost a secondary concern. Such education was to be done by credentialed teachers, not well-meaning outsiders. Until World War I, Cooper's view was dominant in Seattle. With the war, that began to change.

25. Frank Cooper, Letter to Henry R. King, January 6, 1920, SP.

7

World War I: Schooling in Transition, 1917–1918

The American involvement in World War I raised issues that bitterly divided the Seattle school board and changed its prewar understanding of schooling. Before the war, the board had determined school policy with minimal interference from citizens, business groups, levels of government, or the courts. The board had consistently denied access to school buildings and the curriculum to people outside its control. But during World War I, requests from outsiders either came from the United States government or were promoted as part of the larger task of winning a popular war. Questions of patriotism and the uses of money became paramount. Board members disagreed sharply on such issues as the school's role in the war effort, citizen pressures to drop faculty and classes not supportive of the war, and schooling's cost to the taxpayers. These school issues mirrored wartime tensions and changes in the larger society.

When the United States entered World War I on April 6, 1917, the Seattle school board was already split into two factions. A divided board had been unheard of during the previous sixteen years of Cooper's tenure. But with war in Europe, the issues of war-preparedness and a war-minded patriotism permeated American life. Everywhere, people who were politically "left wing" and who opposed entry into the war were called "unpatriotic" by those who were politically more conservative. In Seattle, progressives, labor union men, and Socialists were all vulnerable on the issue of patriotism.[1]

1. See H. C. Peterson and Gilbert Fite, *Opponents of War, 1917–1918* (Madison: University of Wisconsin Press, 1957).

Since January 1917 the school board had often voted three to two on issues. Nathan Eckstein, prominent German-American business-man, led the pro-war, establishment position. He was joined by veteran board members Ebenezer Shorrock, an immigrant banker from England, and George Spencer, a real estate and insurance man. With war-related issues coming regularly to the board, So-cialist Richard Winsor was often sharply at odds with the majority. He was joined by Anna Louise Strong, the real catalyst in board politics.

Anna Louise Strong was unlike all previous board members in many ways. Not only was she the only elected woman in the Cooper years, but she was younger (thirty-one years old) than any board member had been, was unmarried, and had lived only briefly in Seattle—most recently for only three months. Her father, the Rever-end Sydney Strong, was a well-known Seattle clergyman. While board members commonly were well educated, Strong was the only one in Cooper's era with a Ph.D. After graduating from the Univer-sity of Chicago in 1908, she had edited a Protestant weekly. Between 1910–1912 she had organized child-welfare exhibits in various cities for the federal government's new Children's Bureau. Anna Louise Strong was little known in Seattle and was perceived by voters as a child advocate.

Strong was elected in 1916 because few establishment voters both-ered to vote. They assumed her opponent, steel executive George Danz, would be easily elected along with Nathan Eckstein. As noted earlier, women had regularly run for the school board but had never won—despite impressive credentials, organized backing, and wom-en's right to vote for school directors since 1904. The 1916 election had no important school or port issues to get out the vote, and the *Seattle Times* did not wave the red flag vigorously. The *Times* really did not pay much attention to Strong, referring to her as a "well-known child welfare worker." The *Argus* expressed mild concern, because Socialists and women would vote for her. Meanwhile, labor promoted Strong vigorously, with big coverage in the *Seattle Union-Record* and an endorsement from the central labor council. Strong advocated little more than opening schools as community centers ("an experiment in constructive democracy"), and she favored school gardens, supervised playfields, and physical training.[2]

During Strong's brief fifteen months on the board, the style of doing board business changed dramatically. Strong voted "no" more often than all the "no" votes combined in Cooper's preceding sixteen years. She also offered more substitute motions than had been previously offered. Winsor and Strong led the opposition to the military in the schools. They did not fire teachers suspected of disloyalty with the same zeal as did the majority of the board. They voted to retain German in the foreign language curriculum, they voted for a set of controversial history textbooks, and they supported equal pay for women teachers. These were key wartime school issues.

Pressure on the board to allow military training in high schools paralleled the surge of interest in "preparedness" in the larger society. In 1915 the board considered offering military training in the high schools. Socialist Winsor wrote a committee report to the board which concluded that since "no person having conscientious scruples against bearing arms, can be compelled to do military duty in times of peace, that this board should decline to attempt to exercise any power in the premises until authorized and commanded by the laws of this state."[3] The board agreed and kept military training out of the curriculum.

The pressure for and against military training intensified in the spring of 1916. The *Seattle Times* stridently promoted a preparedness campaign, with the schools expected to play a role. With Winsor voting against, the board allowed a National Guard recruiter to speak to high school students. Two days later, the state Parent-Teacher Association resolved to oppose "any attempt to enforce military training upon our public schools." They supported improved physical education, but not military training. Indeed, this resolution encouraged mothers to "study the conditions leading up to war—

2. *Seattle Times*, December 1, 1916, p. 6 (Danz); ibid., p. 1 (Strong); *Seattle Union Record*, December 2, 1916, p. 1 (platform).
3. Minutes of Board, January 7, 1916.

social, political and economic—and the means through which brotherhood may be furthered and future wars avoided."[4]

Two items at the May 24, 1916, board meeting illustrate the conflicting wartime pressures on the board. The Federation of Women's Clubs protested against "military addresses . . . or any addresses of a political nature" in the schools. Then, the Northwest Business Men's Preparedness League requested that school children be organized to march in a preparedness parade. The board relied on past policy and refused.[5] But considerable opposition now threatened the board's long-standing policy of keeping all outside causes and groups out of school life. While some citizens' groups advocated that the schools stay out of all controversy, others just as strongly urged that the schools initiate preparedness.

There was also pressure for military preparedness from within the district administration, most notably from Medical Inspector Ira C. Brown, a member of the Army Officers' Medical Reserve Corps. Brown wanted improved physical education for high school students. By this, he did not mean sports, but rather physical conditioning and marching drill. His motives were mixed. Brown supported an expanded physical education training program not only because it was healthy for students but also because it was preparation for military physical training.

Brown persuaded the board to approve physical training for Ballard High School students and to hire an army lieutenant to lead the program. For fall 1916 the board established physical training in all grade schools, and then agreed to have physical training for all students in all grades. This was the start of all students' taking physical education class. The board also agreed not to use the word "military" in connection with physical training. To some, like the parent who thanked the board for this "Military Training," this class was war preparedness. To others, it was no more than a way to improve the physical well-being of all students. Brown did not speak for all school administrators in wanting to promote preparedness. A Christmas 1916 article in the *Seattle School Bulletin* revealed deeply

4. Resolution, April 7, 1916, SP, Folder "Military Training."
5. Minutes of Board, May 24, 1916.

held feelings against war preparedness. The writer commented on the preponderance of war toys available locally, and expressing disapproval, concluded: "The school shops have sought to have the wonderful achievements of peace the motive prompting the boy in his creation of things he likes to make."[6]

War preparedness manifested itself in two other indicators of patriotism—the citizenship of teachers, and flag saluting. The board asked if any teachers were not citizens, and if such teachers planned to become citizens. This request was initiated by Richard Winsor, who was feeling pressure because of his opposition to the military in schools. With this resolution, Winsor hoped to remind his critics that a Socialist could also be a loyal American. Additionally, few schoolrooms had American flags. Participation in a flag-saluting ritual was rare. In the several years surrounding the American involvement in World War I, however, that changed. The board placed American flags in classrooms, and flag-saluting exercises became common.[7]

The resistance of school districts like Seattle to military training resulted in efforts during the 1917 state legislature to compel military training statewide in high schools. Anna Louise Strong countered by offering at her first board meeting a resolution against such attempts. Strong moved "that the board go on record as opposed to any bill which transfers to any military authority directly or indirectly, any legal control direct or advisory over any course of training or the personnel of any group of instructors in the public schools." Only Strong and Winsor voted for this resolution. The entire board, however, agreed throughout the war that school officials would not cooperate with recruiters or the draft.[8]

Promptly after the United States entered the war on April 6, 1917,

6. Ibid., August 14, 1916 (grade schools); ibid., January 8, 1917 (physical training); ibid., March 7, 1916 (parent); *Seattle School Bulletin*, December 1916, pp. 3, 4 (war toys).

7. Minutes of Board, June 7, 1916 (citizenship). In 1919 the state legislature made citizenship a requirement for teaching in Washington. *Seattle School Bulletin*, December 1915, p. 3 (flag saluting); Frank Cooper, Memorandum to School Board, February 28, 1919, SP; Minutes of Board, October 25, 1918.

8. Minutes of Board, January 12, 1917 (Strong); ibid., May 1, 1917 (board refusal).

requests came to the board for voluntary military drill groups. In response, the board considered the United States Army's after-school
military drill program in lieu of physical education class. Dr. Brown
volunteered to be in charge.

Despite the fact that war had been declared, Cooper boldly opposed this military training, concluding that "it is not a good time to
undertake to establish military training in a public high school."
Cooper strongly urged that School Guards "should not be accepted
nor adopted as a permanent school policy." He did not want students to wear uniforms to school because "it raises a class distinction
and is undemocratic in its effects." He cautioned that it would be
hard to find rooms for the program at a time when buildings were
crowded anyway. And he wondered if the drill should be two days
per week (the state requirement for physical education) or three
days per week (the U. S. Army requirement for the program).[9] These
practical objections, however, were not Cooper's real concerns.

Cooper felt the School Guard proposal raised two fundamental
questions. First, he wondered "whether military training is a branch
of instruction entitled to be considered in the same light as any other
study or subject, and if it is so considered, whether it should not be
given the same recognition by being placed upon the elective list of
subjects." Second, he asked "whether, if it is allowed that military
training has sufficient educative value to be given recognition along
with other branches of instruction, there may be reasons concerned
with the public good or affecting public policy sufficient to outweigh
its claims to a place in a public school course."[10] Despite this opposition from its superintendent, the board majority voted to allow the
School Guards, with Strong and Winsor voting against.

Some prewar policies central to the board's understanding of
schooling were changed during the war, not to be reenacted afterward with the same vigor. A basic prewar policy had kept outside
agencies, groups, and businesses out of schools. This ban on outsiders was first violated when the board allowed sewing classes to
make items for the Red Cross. Subsequently, the board allowed the

9. Frank Cooper, Memorandum to School Board, April 23, 1917, SP, Folder "Military Training."
10. Ibid., April 23, 1917.

Harvesters' League to recruit boys for summer farm work. They then permitted the Central Council of Patriotic Services to sponsor a program in the schools on Conscription Day.

The board also dropped its long-standing opposition to fund drives. Students were encouraged to practice self-denial and to contribute money at school for war relief or buy Liberty Bonds. Home economics classes participated in government campaigns to save food ("Hooverizing"), use the "lowly potato," teach adult women to conserve, and can fruits and vegetables for the war. The school garden program became part of "The United States School Garden Army."[11]

With the war, the first instance of the federal government's influencing the curriculum occurred through the Smith-Hughes Vocational Act. Under this act, the federal government paid school districts to offer vocational classes. In Seattle, that meant adult night classes relating to war needs: shipbuilding and radio. A. L. Brown, Seattle's supervisor of evening schools, told the board that the high schools were inadequately built to handle the demand for vocational rather than academic work. Men did not want classes in wood shop, he said, but rather machine, gas-engine, sheet metal, and auto-repair shops. "They are asking for real vocational work," he concluded. Jobs existed in the local economy, adults wanted the training to get the jobs, and they looked to the school system to provide it. Because the Smith-Hughes Vocational Act required the participation of organized labor in planning the curriculum, the Seattle schools began to cooperate with the Seattle Central Labor Council on the question of adult vocational education.[12]

The problem of low teachers' salaries became acute in the spring

11. Minutes of Board, October 23, 1917 (liberty bonds); F. Hopkins, Memorandum to Frank Cooper, July 9, 1918, SP, Folder "Home Economics" (home economics); *Seattle School Bulletin*, May 1918, pp. 1, 2; *Quinquennial Report*, 1916–1921, p. 76 (gardening).

12. A. L. Brown, Memorandum to Frank Cooper, February 15, 1918, SP. Congress passed the Smith-Hughes Vocational Act on February 23, 1917. The Washington state legislature passed legislation on March 17, 1917, allowing school districts to use Smith-Hughes funds. The state plan was approved on December 14, 1917. On the Smith-Hughes Vocational Act and labor's cooperation with the Seattle schools, see Daniel Jacoby, "Schools, Unions, and Training: Seattle, 1900–1940" (Ph.D. diss., University of Washington, 1986).

of 1917. War industry in Seattle had quickly attracted workers, especially in the shipyards, with the result that wages and prices were seriously inflated. The school board tried to control expenditures, while the teachers tried to keep up with inflation. Inflation won. Teachers had continually sought to raise the status of teaching to a career choice for educated, competent people. Now they had to struggle not to be forced out of teaching because of low salaries, and to keep close to the rate of inflation. In the first few months of the war, this effort took the form of teachers' asking for salary increases and establishing a retirement system.

In the spring of 1917, the board discussed saving money by dropping salary credit for teaching experience gained elsewhere. Cooper strongly supported salary credit for such experience. He cautioned that such a move would "lower in a more marked degree the teaching and professional average of your corps of teachers. The excellent quality of the teacher supply will inevitably be reduced by our failure to credit." Then he observed why Seattle had developed such a good teaching corps: "We have been demanding teachers who have reached a high standard of efficiency and we have been able to get them because of our location, our standards and our equal or better salary schedule." He argued that instead of lowering salaries by not giving credit for previous work, that "more liberality should be exercised, because we are often not able to get the best candidates at the present maximum for new teachers, particularly in the case of men."[13]

The inflationary pressures of the Seattle war economy necessitated constant requests from teachers for raises. Rather than uniting, however, the teachers fragmented into subgroups organized by grade level, subject specialty, length of service, and sex. Each subgroup looked out for itself. These balkanized teachers had so little power that a successful strike for higher wages was unthinkable.

The most desperate teachers were those least likely to find remunerative white-collar jobs in the war industry—the women grade school teachers just beginning to teach in Seattle. These women or-

13. Frank Cooper, Memorandum to School Board, May 9, 1917, SP, Folder "Salaries."

ganized themselves into a "Committee of Minimum Teachers" and, in a memorandum to Cooper, described their financial plight as revealed through a questionnaire. These teachers commonly lived in rented quarters with meals provided. Some did all their own cooking, but reported that they would rather not, "because the time thus used is needed for school work or recreation." Others had to live at home or with relatives. For room and board, the average expenditure was $37.50. All were apprehensive about an upcoming monthly rent increase of from $5.00 to $10.00. For laundry, including having clothes cleaned, they spent $3.86 per month, noting that because of the "oiled floors and the chalk dust in the room, this cleaning must be done." They spent $3.06 on carfare, which included not only the daily commute to school but the four to eight meetings each month required of new teachers. Some teachers carried insurance, costing an average of $5.60 per month. Most carried no insurance, and "several have been compelled to drop this protection since September. . . . Furthermore, the heavy strain of meeting economic problems is making many of them poor risks for insurance companies."

The committee also noted that, because of the expense, "many have dropped all church work. . . . To give is very difficult; to refuse is despicable." The average given for church and charity was $3.80. Many had purchased no new clothing, while others spent $15.00 per month. The teachers spent $3.40 per month on professional expenditures, and the report noted "how very few are able to avail themselves of courses offered in our University." They spent only $1.85 per month on recreation. The committee observed that "many of these new teachers have few if any friends here, and no way of meeting any. Too many of them spend their evenings in loneliness. Deprived of church, clubs, and recreation they lose joy in life and their work assuredly suffers."[14]

In the winter and spring of 1917–1918, proposals for raising teacher salaries were numerous. Proposals included raising the high school differential, paying the high school teachers a bonus during the war, and being flexible in salary for hard-to-fill spots, such as

14. Committee of Minimum Teachers, Memorandum to Frank Cooper, December 15, 1917, SP, Folder "Salaries."

manual training. The *Argus* did not think much of raising teacher salaries, and suggested that teachers work half of the summer for the Red Cross to further the war effort. "The trouble with teachers," it complained, "is that they have had a snap for so long that they do not realize that it is a snap."[15]

A teacher's salary did not include a fringe package of medical, dental, and life insurance, or of retirement benefits. If a teacher wanted insurance, the payments had to come out of salary. Retirement was harder for an individual to finance. Following the national trend, legislation was passed in the summer of 1917 allowing local districts to establish retirement systems. The creation of a retirement system was an important part of the struggle to make teaching a career. Cooper advocated the retirement system to the board as a way to promote "true economy and . . . greater efficiency," because it would provide a way to end humanely the careers of older teachers who wanted to quit.[16] More important, once a retirement fund was established, however meager, it became possible to think of teaching as a career from which one could retire by age seventy and still have an income. Prior to that, few could seriously think about staying in teaching.

By the summer of 1917 Seattle was booming with wartime industry and wartime patriotism. Prominent Socialist and labor leader Hulet Wells had been arrested in May for distributing a pamphlet against the draft. In July the Reverend Sydney Strong, well-known clergyman and father of Anna Louise Strong, was expelled from the Municipal League for speaking against the war. The Municipal League consisted of progressive reformers, but it, too, was severely compromised by wartime patriotic excesses. Throughout the summer, the AFL and the IWW tried to unionize the lumber industry, succeeding in shutting down 75 percent of the industry before the

15. *Argus*, March 23, 1918, p. 1.
16. Frank Cooper, Memorandum to School Board ("A Superintendent's View as to the Advisability of a Retirement Fund for Teachers"), undated, SP, Folder "Retirement Fund." Legislation to establish a teachers' retirement system was passed by the Washington state legislature in 1913 (*Laws of Washington*, 1913, 129, chapter 48, March 11), but was defeated by voters in a referendum on November 3, 1914. Subsequently, the legislature gave first-class districts the right to establish their own retirement systems (*Laws of Washington* 1917, 744, chapter 163, March 16).

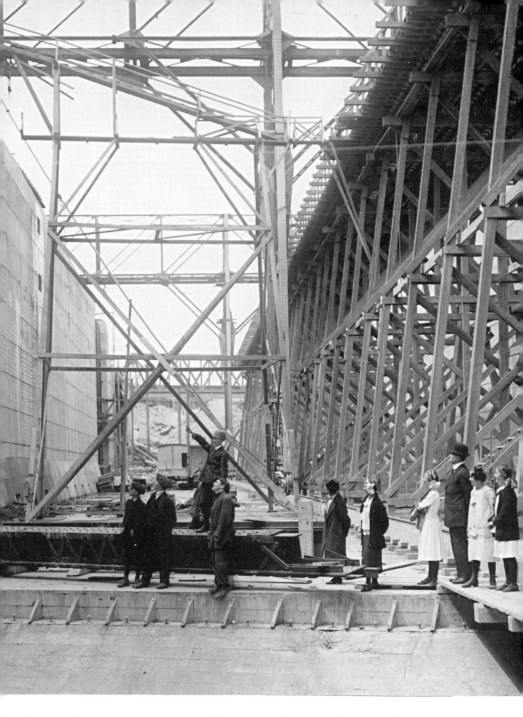

Lawton School field trip to Lake Washington Ship Canal locks under construction, n.d. (*Washington State Historical Society*)

Main Street School, students of Japanese background, 1914. Japanese American students formed the largest minority group in the Seattle schools. Here, students in traditional costume dance on the school grounds. (*Washington State Historical Society*)

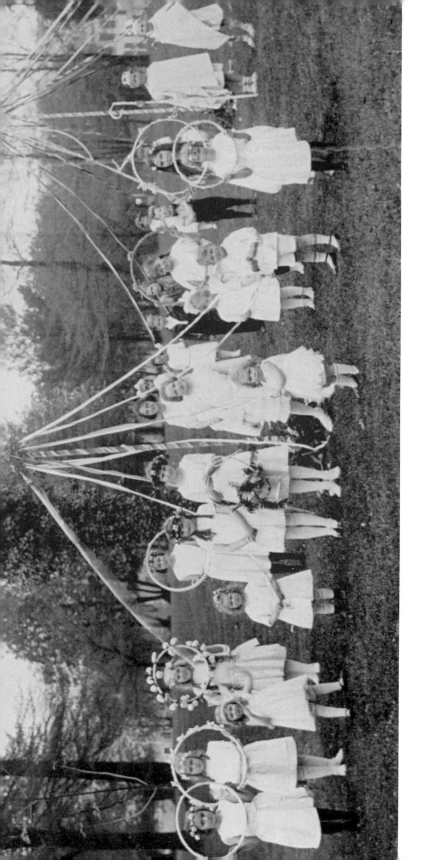

MacDonald School, May Day celebration, 1915. (*Seattle Public School Archives*)

Lincoln High School, senior play, *Mary Jane's Pa*, 1916. (*Seattle Public School Archives*)

West Seattle High School, senior ball, 1914. The issue of whether schools should sponsor dances created more controversy than any other issue prior to World War I. (*Seattle Public School Archives*)

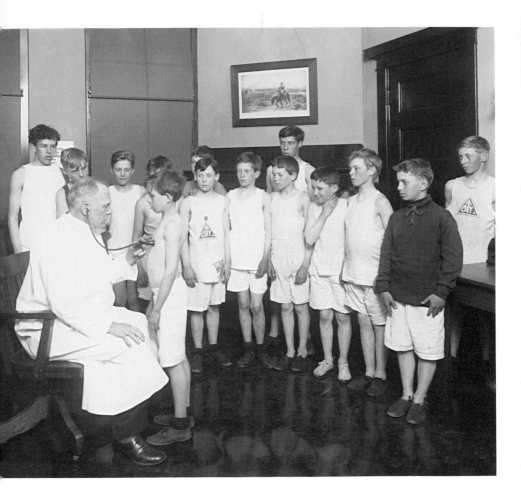

Ira C. Brown, M.D., giving a medical exam, n.d. Dr. Brown was hired in 1914 as the district's medical inspector. (*Washington State Historical Society*)

Seattle Public Schools Clinic, dental operating room, n.d. As part of the district's medical services, dental work was provided at the district clinic for needy students. (*Washington State Historical Society*)

Milk break, n.d. In 1915 the district started distributing milk for free (or at minimal cost) in order to improve the health of many children. (*Seattle Public School Archives*)

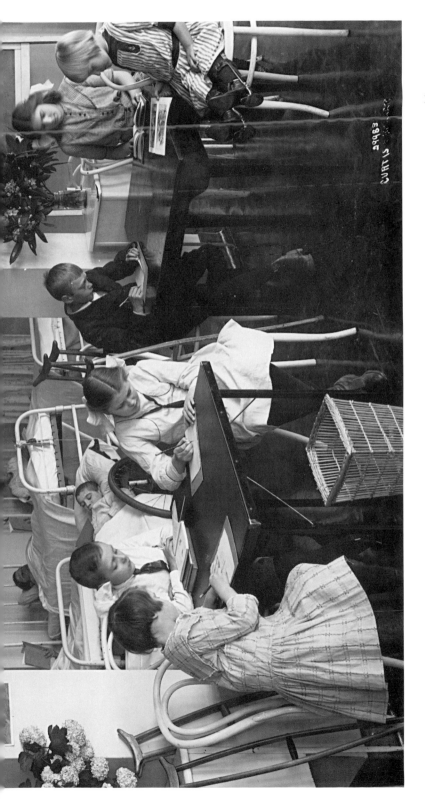

Children's Orthopedic Hospital, children with teacher, n.d. The district provided teachers for children in nonpublic institutions, such as Children's Orthopedic Hospital. (*Washington State Historical Society*)

Boys' Parental School, students playing marbles, n.d. Young adolescent boys who were troublesome in their neighborhoods were sent to the district's custodial school, the Boys' Parental School (later named Luther Burbank School) on Mercer Island. (*Seattle Public School Archives*)

Girls' Parental School, students playing baseball, n.d. Girls with tendencies toward delinquency were sent to the Girls' Parental School (later named Martha Washington School) at Brighton Beach on Lake Washington. (*Seattle Public School Archives*)

Broadway High School, chemistry class, n.d. High school academic classes were offered to adults in the evening. *(Seattle Public School Archives)*

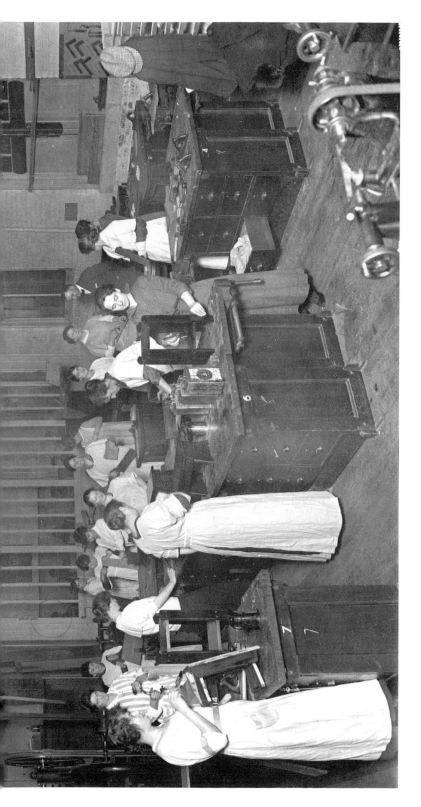

Broadway High School, women's carpentry class, n.d. Evening school featured a wide range of practical and academic classes. (*Seattle Public School Archives*)

West Seattle High School, business machines class, n.d. Commercial classes were very popular in Seattle, often leading to jobs in Seattle's burgeoning office force. (*Seattle Public School Archives*)

B. F. Day School, students knitting, 1916. During World War I students were often mobilized to work on projects for the war effort. (*Seattle Public School Archives*)

Adams School, flag salute, n.d. With World War I, the ritual of saluting the flag became important, and the district started to place American flags in all classrooms. (*Seattle Public School Archives*)

strikes failed in the fall. The personal consequences of being politically radical, or of being opposed to the war, were becoming more onerous in Seattle. It grew worse for such people when the federal government moved against the Wobblies (IWW) and the Socialists with the new Espionage Act.

In Seattle, a volunteer civilian group called the "Minute Men" set the tone for patriotic activity. Led by prominent civic leader Thomas Burke, the Minute Men became the local division of a national group, the American Protective League (APL). The APL operated with the official support of the United States Department of Justice, calling themselves "THE MEN BEHIND THE GOVERNMENT." The Minute Men application form described their purpose as "suppressing sedition and treason and efforts to embarrass the government in the prosecution of our present war."[17] The Minute Men focused their attention on draft dodgers, the Wobblies, and any labor groups considered radical. They also acted as a patriotic pressure group on the schools, attempting to eliminate any radical or pro-German influences. Many Seattle Minute Men were Spanish-American War veterans.

The school activities of the Minute Men centered on four issues. First, they were often involved in successful attempts to fire teachers who were unsupportive of the war. Second, they were prominent in the recall of board member Anna Louise Strong. Third, they led the drive to drop German as an elective foreign language. And fourth, they led the drive to drop certain textbooks thought to be pro-German.

In August 1917 pressure was first put on the school board to fire faculty who gave less than full support to the American war effort. Before the war, outsiders had made no demands that faculty be fired for political reasons. But with the changed political climate, teachers were vulnerable to purges. Teachers were vulnerable not only because they were public employees with no rights of job security but also because they were viewed as shapers of opinion among young people. The ease with which teachers were intimidated and fired

17. Seattle, University of Washington Libraries (UWL), Vertical File 301, Folder "American Protective League, Minute Men Division, Seattle."

underscored both the wartime excesses in Seattle and the hopelessly dependent, vulnerable position of teachers.

School administrators did not defend "free speech" or "due process" for faculty, in part because administrators were just as vulnerable as teachers. The board had the right to hire and fire "at its pleasure," and the voters could do as they pleased with board members. As will be noted, one board member who resisted the firings, Anna Louise Strong, was recalled. The other, Richard Winsor, was defeated for reelection in 1920 by a man who was associated with wartime patriotic groups. School board members, administrators, and teachers were all expected to provide patriotic leadership, not wartime dissent.

Teachers were expected to project a certain ideal. When doubt was cast on a teacher, and that teacher became an object of controversy, then that teacher was dismissed. The firing of H. F. W. Kilian, a teacher of German at Broadway High School, typifies the pressure under which educators worked. The Seattle Minute Men had probably first raised the question of Kilian's fitness, as the board received a formal complaint on Kilian from Acting Director Charles Petrovitsky of the United States Department of Justice. Petrovitsky complained of Kilian's "pro-German proclivities." Kilian's position was that "the acts of Germany were not acts of war against the U.S. . . . therefore, the United States was not justified in entering the war."

A school board subcommittee reported that "at best, Mr. Kilian considered both sides equally to blame, in contrast with the declaration of the President." The subcommittee felt that by finding fault on both sides, Kilian was no longer a convincing model of patriotism for his students. The subcommittee noted: "Mr. Kilian apparently failed to appreciate the fact that the School Code provides that a teacher must teach patriotism, and the rights and duties of American citizens and that on the contrary, his attitude and utterances have been condemnatory as to the United States, and apologetic as to Germany."

For a teacher, being neutral or even quiet about wartime issues was unacceptable. A teacher was obliged to teach "morals, patriotism and civic duty as an integral part of the curriculum. . . . Teaching

118

which is not positive, forceful and whole-hearted is worse than useless, as such teaching can only spring from conviction and cannot be made to order." Teachers did not have the luxury of being aloof from the war: "What could be tolerated in the ordinary avocations of life cannot be tolerated in an instructor of the young. . . . At best, Mr. Kilian is neutral."[18]

Because Kilian claimed neutrality, yet lost his job, it became easier for patriotic groups such as the Minute Men to go after other teachers. A total of six teachers were fired, with one reinstated. The validity of the charges against the teachers became a secondary consideration. Indeed, the fact that charges were brought was sufficient to taint a teacher so that the teacher was considered incapable of exerting a positive influence on students.

The Minute Men were not sure about Superintendent Cooper's patriotism, but they never brought formal charges. They did not like his friendship with Queen Anne High School Principal Otto Luther, whose wartime patriotism was also suspect. They wondered why teachers of German replaced other capable teachers after German was dropped. When Cooper told teachers not to push for total student participation in the Thrift Stamp drive, they wondered why Cooper did not want to discover which students were not contributing (i.e., were unpatriotic). A Minute Men report noted that "these would be just the pupils that the school would wish to unearth and to correct, and, if possible, to transform into patriotic pupils." And they wondered why he defended not only the teaching of German but also use of the tainted Ginn history textbooks.[19]

In December 1917 organized labor looked to the school board and port elections as a tune-up for the upcoming May municipal election. Organized labor was very strong in Seattle, in part because the federal government supported wartime unionization in key industries to ensure stability. In the week of the December elections, newspaper headlines announced that 20,000 more shipbuilding jobs would be created. The time looked right for labor to flex its political muscles. Labor ran Charles Doyle against the board's fiscal expert,

18. Minutes of Board, December 29, 1917.
19. Seattle, UWL, Thomas Burke Papers, 33-7, Folder "American Protective League," 1918–1919."

Ebenezer Shorrock. Doyle was a veteran labor leader and an important member of the Central Labor Council. Despite the *Seattle Union Record*'s high hopes and best efforts, Shorrock trounced Doyle. Socialist Richard Winsor, however, was reelected. Had Doyle won, he, Winsor, and Strong would have formed a wartime school board majority sympathetic to labor. Instead, school politics became markedly more conservative.

The day after the election, the *Seattle Times* commented editorially that "public sentiment, as revealed by the results of these two elections, unquestionably is inclining at this time toward a very marked conservatism. . . . It indicates that recent events, local, national and international, have exercised a sobering influence upon all public thought." The downtown *Argus* grumped about the social and political price to be paid for wartime prosperity, warning:

> Do not underestimate the forces with which decency has to contend. The United States authorities tell us that this is a hotbed of pro-Germanism. We know that the IWW are thicker than flies around a stable. Lewd women and their consorts are here in alarming numbers. It is a bootlegger's paradise. Add to this element a lot of addle-pated people who want to do right, but have not the ability to distinguish the good from the bad, and there is no telling what will happen.[20]

The specter of increased vice and radical political activity was sobering to a patriotic, conservative element in Seattle. In response, the United Spanish-American War Veterans spent election day outside voting places gathering signatures to conduct a recall election of Anna Louise Strong.

Anna Louise Strong looked like an unpatriotic school board member to the veterans. Her father was an outspoken opponent of the war, and she had written against the draft three weeks before the Conscription Act was passed, had written columns in the *Seattle Union Record* against the war, and had testified in defense of Hulet

20. *Seattle Times*, December 2, 1917, p. 6; *Argus*, December 8, 1917, p. 1.

Wells at his first espionage trial. Strong wrote about this trial in her autobiography: "After it I was the best-known woman in Seattle; I was no longer among the most respectable."[21]

The signature drive to recall Strong faltered after the Hulet Wells trial, and indeed it might have died. Harvey O'Connor recalled the story of a woman passing the recall headquarters and asking why Strong was being recalled: " 'She's against the war,' came the answer. 'My God, who isn't?' said the woman, and passed on." By her own admission, however, Strong sparked renewed interest in her recall by showing sympathy for Louise Olivereau, an IWW secretary also on trial for violating the Espionage Act. Olivereau had mailed statements to Seattle draftees, encouraging them to resist the draft. At her trial, Olivereau proclaimed herself an anarchist. She refused an attorney, but asked that Strong sit next to her. Strong did so. When Olivereau was convicted, the patriotic groups stepped up their recall petition drive against Strong. The *Argus* called on Strong to "have the decency to resign from the school board, without putting the community to the expense of holding an election which can by no possibility result otherwise than in her removal. . . . The sooner that Anna Strong is dispensed with as a school director the better."[22]

The Strong recall election was held with the March 5, 1918, mayoralty election. The pre-election press coverage of the Strong recall was minimal, focusing instead on the mayoralty contest between Ole Hanson and James Bradford. Hanson portrayed the election as a plebiscite on the Americanism of the candidates. Patriotism was very much in the news. One week before the election, a grand jury in Seattle began investigating fifty-seven cases of treason and sedition. Three days before the election, the Department of Labor ordered that some Pacific Northwest Wobblies be rounded up and deported. Given this context, the newspapers did not have to advocate the defeat of Anna Louise Strong. Afterward, the *Seattle Times* gloated:

21. Strong, *I Change Worlds*, p. 63.
22. O'Connor, *Revolution in Seattle*, p. 102; Strong, *I Change Worlds*, p. 63; *Argus*, December 8, 1917, p. 1.

Anna Louise Strong, in spite of the consolidation in her behalf of every IWW, every Red Socialist, every pacifist, every man and woman who disapproves of the recall principle, and the large numbers who came to her aid through mistaken sympathy for a woman, was ejected from office with most creditable neatness and dispatch. The sound of the door to public favor locking behind her will be music in the ears of the Seattle boys who have already reached the trenches in France.[23]

Anna Louise Strong was recalled after only fifteen months on the board, but the margin was fairly close. She lost by 5,720 votes—27,167 for recall to 21,447 against. Ole Hanson beat James Bradford for mayor—32,202 to 27,683. While it was noteworthy that Strong was recalled, it was equally noteworthy that the voters were closely divided. Many who voted in the mayoralty election did not mark their ballots in Strong's recall. Voting on school questions was always limited to a minority special-interest group that felt itself to have a vital stake in the schools.

There was another reason for Strong's recall, quite unrelated to war but important in the context of wartime patriotism. Strong had become an outsider to the women and men active in school politics. The Federation of Women's Clubs, the Parent-Teacher Association, the University Women's Club, and the Municipal League had all urged her recall. Strong was all too unlike the society women, PTA mothers, lawyers, doctors, and businessmen active in school issues. By comparison, she was a little old still to be unmarried, and she was highly educated, independent, and nomadic. As the daughter of a social-activist clergyman, she was attracted to labor, the Socialists, and groups opposed to American involvement in World War I. Strong confided in her autobiography: "I did not greatly care about the outcome of the recall; I hated those meetings of the School Board."[24]

After Strong was recalled, she came to the next board meeting and made a statement asking that a woman be appointed her successor.

23. *Seattle Times*, March 6, 1918, p. 6.
24. Strong, *I Change Worlds*, p. 65.

Other groups attended, also asking that a woman be appointed, but not a woman like Strong. One delegation urged that a woman be appointed, but "that the woman should be a mother, and preferably one with children in the schools, whose patriotism is absolutely unquestioned."[25] The seven names suggested for a replacement were women of which the club and PTA women would approve. The board appointed a prominent club woman, Evangeline C. Harper, to Strong's seat.

A third area of concern for the United Spanish-American War Veterans, acting through the Minute Men, was the teaching of German as an elective foreign-language class. Cooper was not intimidated by such protests and staunchly supported the teaching of German, saying, "It is required for entrance to certain courses in the colleges and universities and it embodies a very rich literature of science and its applications." He noted that, after the war, American leaders in industry and commerce would need to know German to compete with the Germans: "Because we are at war with a nation is not a sufficient reason for our depriving our youth of the advantages of as complete equipment as we can give them for the demands of their day and generation. . . . Aversion to and detestation of things German may carry us to unreasonable and to reactionary limits." Cooper acknowledged, however, that German could be dropped under public pressure. "If the time comes," Cooper wrote, "that public heat against the German language becomes at all intense, it would be better to drop it because of the unnatural fever, but for no other reasons."[26]

The "unnatural fever" worsened. Protests after Cooper's defense of German came from the United Spanish-American War Veterans and others. John W. Roberts replied to Cooper's defense: "I have been wondering why I should go without bacon as I have for the last six months, while contributing money toward the teaching of German, which is certainly non-essential, if not unpatriotic, at this time." Roberts then asked Cooper how much it cost to teach Ger-

25. Minutes of Board, March 7, 1918.
26. Frank Cooper, Memorandum to School Board, January 7, 1918, SP, Folder "Foreign Language."

man. With this question, German immigrant board member Nathan Eckstein was in a tough spot. While he probably disliked letting outside pressure groups force a change in board policy, Eckstein also had to keep anti-German pressure groups from hurting his family's business. A staunch naturalized American, Eckstein voted to drop German. Then, right after Anna Louise Strong was recalled, the board asked Cooper how many students wanted the class for the following year. Cost and benefit quickly replaced Cooper's principled defense as the basis for retaining German. With the still-vivid example of Strong's recall, the firing of some teachers, and an ongoing textbook controversy, Cooper yielded to the pressure. In April 1918 he recommended dropping German.[27]

In the summer of 1918 a simmering controversy heated up over history textbooks. Cooper, along with high school principals and history teachers, had tried since 1914 to persuade the board to purchase the Ginn three-volume *Outlines of European History* by James Breasted, James Harvey Robinson, and Charles Beard. School boards nationally were having problems with these textbooks. The books were alleged to be pro-German and the patriotism of the authors was suspect. Beard was on a list of German sympathizers, and Robinson had contributed $100 to a Wobblies' defense fund. Additionally, the fact that Ginn had modified volume two was seen by critics as an admission by Ginn that the series was indeed tainted.

In Seattle, this refusal by the lay board members to adopt the text-

27. See Minutes of Board for January 21, 1918, January 19, 1918, and March 18, 1918 (protests); John Roberts, Letter to Frank Cooper, January 15, 1918. Seattle, UWL, Thomas Burke Papers, 33-7, Folder "American Protective League, 1918–1919." Cooper said his earlier reasons for retaining German ("founded upon cultural and commercial demands") were still valid, but that, in addition to "public heat," he would recommend dropping German for one other reason: "I believe there has been an organized attempt on the part of the Prussian element in this country that has resisted complete Americanization, to foster and to promote the extension of German ideals and German influence in this country" (Frank Cooper, Memorandum to School Board, April 1, 1918, SP, Folder "Foreign Language"). German language class was effectively eliminated during World War I from high schools nationally. In 1915, 24.4% of all high school students took German, but in 1922 less than 1% took German. Edward A. Krug, *The Shaping of the American High School, 1880–1920* (New York: Harper and Row, 1964), p. 407.

books recommended by the educators greatly irritated Cooper. He was the advocate for the teachers, and he knew how essential were new books. The Ginn series emphasized modern Europe rather than the classical world, something the moribund history program needed. Cooper admonished the board by saying, "It will be generally felt by the high school principals and teachers that a great waste of effort will be entailed, and that the work in this subject will suffer so seriously that it might be almost as well for the board to abandon the work in general history in the high schools until such time as the board may think it advisable to purchase the recommended and adopted books."[28]

In coming weeks, the relationship between Cooper and the board worsened because of the textbook issue. At the August 6 meeting, Cooper challenged the board to buy the Ginn books or drop history. He castigated the board for stalling and for buckling to patriotic pressure groups:

> May I not suggest that there are deeper questions involved in this matter than that of the expenditure of $2,000, and they are of extreme moment. One of them . . . is whether the judgment of a professional group upon a professional question is worth while, and when that judgment has been deliberately reached and expressed, whether it is in the interests of the schools to have it ignored or negated.[29]

In an unprecedented move, the board formed an outside committee of six prominent citizens to examine the Ginn textbooks for pro-German bias. This textbook committee subsequently advised the board not to buy the Ginn series until the new edition was available for examination. Committee members Thomas Burke and J. T. Jennings suggested that the district continue to use the old textbooks and "the various pamphlets on the war issued under the auspices of

28. Frank Cooper, Memorandum to School Board, July 30, 1918, SP, Folder "Textbook Commission, 1921–1923." This memorandum was read at the August 6, 1918, board meeting.
29. Ibid., August 6, 1918, SP, Folder "Textbook Commission, 1921–1923."

the U.S. government."[30] The board chose to wait and reexamine the revised edition.

In addition to patriotism, the other important wartime issue for the board was money—specifically, teacher salary requests to keep up with wartime inflation. Not only were teachers leaving for higher paying jobs, but, among applicants, there were not many men teachers from which to choose. One plan to attract men was to pay them a wartime bonus. Cooper opposed this because it would be perceived by women teachers as discriminatory and unfair and would be harmful to morale and efficiency. Salaries, he believed, should not be based "upon anything but service." He also opposed a wartime bonus to help those with dependents, even if applied equally to men and women, and even if paid the same to those with the same number of dependents. It would "result in bad feeling in the corps," declared Cooper, "because there are single men without dependents, who are recognized as being superior in service to some men having dependents, and the same is true of the women."[31]

In the spring of 1918 Cooper asked the board to set a wartime salary bonus. He proposed raising the pay of everyone "in order to make the pay of the lowest salaried teachers consistent with adequacy in normal times." A norm would then be determined for living at that standard in these "abnormal" times, and a bonus would be paid to those below that amount. All of this was to be temporary—only for the duration of "the present excessive cost of living." In the spring of 1918 all teachers except the 152 women high school teachers received a wartime bonus. The High School Teachers' League promptly opposed this discrimination against its women members, and the state Federation of Women's Clubs fumed:

> The plea that men should have more because they could make more as plumbers is no longer tenable, as business opportunities

30. Minutes of Board, September 24, 1918.

31. Frank Cooper, Memorandum to School Board, January 22, 1918, SP, Folder "Salaries." The results of a questionnaire asking how many teachers had dependents were summarized in a November 7, 1917, report. Of the 246 respondents, 91 were married with someone at least partially dependent. Of the 155 unmarried, only 36 had no dependents.

for women are constantly offering more incomes than teaching, and even as mechanics the world war has shown the ability and capacity of women.

In July the board gave bonuses to janitors, engineers, and firemen.[32]

During the summer of 1918 the board agreed to examine the question of salary differences between groups of teachers. A number of groups or individuals supported "equal pay for equal work" for men and women teachers. The salary-bonus issue would not be settled until after the December school board election. The men high school teachers requested of the new board that the same $300 bonus be paid to their women colleagues. Undoubtedly the board's treatment of women high school teachers had caused a morale problem among all teachers. If one group of teachers could be treated with disdain by an intransigent board, then surely other high-handed actions could follow. Some board members had dug in their heels and had chosen this issue to "make a stand" against pressure by teachers. The board approved the bonus for women. In February 1919 an "equal pay for equal work" bill became state law.[33]

In the meantime, another concern dwarfed all other issues: namely, several major influenza epidemics.[34] On two occasions in 1918, influenza was particularly virulent in Seattle—from mid-October to mid-November, and during the last few weeks of December. Without vaccines, and because of the varieties of influenza, the only way to control an influenza outbreak was to reduce contact between people. Such tactics required cooperation between medical and political leaders, and a willingness by all citizens to alter daily routines.

With the influenza epidemics, the school and city health boards

32. Frank Cooper, Memorandum to School Board, April 19, 1918, SP, Folder "Salaries"; *Legislative Counsellor*, 3, no. 5 (May 1918): 8; Minutes of Board, July 17, 1918.

33. *Legislative Counsellor* 3, no. 5 (May 1918): 8 (male teachers' request); *Laws of Washington*, 1919, 55, chapter 27, February 14.

34. For the Seattle epidemics, see Nancy Rockafellar, "Public Health in Progressive Seattle, 1876–1919" (M.A. thesis, University of Washington, 1986); idem, " 'In Gauze We Trust': Public Health and Spanish Influenza on the Home Front, Seattle, 1918–1919," *Pacific Northwest Quarterly* 77, no. 3 (July 1986): 104–13.

had to work closely together in the first instance of cooperation since the school board had reorganized its medical work independent of the city's Board of Health in 1913. Throughout October, November, and December of 1918, the constant question before the school board was whether to close schools. The school board tried to make its decisions by relying on Dr. Brown, the school nurses, the city's Board of Health, and various medical doctors.

The Seattle schools closed in the second week of October and re-opened on November 14, 1918, losing twenty-eight school days. Even after reopening, the absentee rate remained high. School nurses, doctors throughout the city, and the city health commis-sioner reported a considerable sickness around the city, but not all of it influenza. Cooper advised the board that several schools were missing one-third to one-half of their students, that nurses were overwhelmed, that information on the nature of the illness was not reliable, that the number of influenza cases was small, that teacher absenteeism had been high, and that five teachers had died. Taking the advice of eleven doctors, the board extended Christmas vacation and closed schools between December 13–30, 1918. Dr. Brown urged that the board do something to keep students off the streets, be-cause "the value of the closing of the schools at this time in connec-tion with the epidemic is being nullified by children of school age being permitted on downtown streets and in places of public assem-bly." The board also forbade teachers to take other jobs during the closure, "to protect teachers from contagion."[35]

The pall cast over Seattle in the winter of 1918–1919 by deadly in-fluenza epidemics was but one more grim reminder that the Ameri-can involvement in World War I had profoundly changed Seattle. In-flation, labor unrest, an influx of wartime workers, the strength of the Minute Men, strident patriotic politics, newspaper bombast about winning the war, and many other wartime events and trends—all combined to make the mood in Seattle very different from what it had been before April 1917. In short, World War I had

35. Minutes of Board, December 20, 1918; ibid., December 18, 1918.

effectively disrupted the agenda of prewar progressivism throughout America, and Seattle was no exception.[36]

The Seattle public schools were significantly altered by World War
I, with the war years serving as a transition period between the prewar progressive view of schooling and a more conservative view in
the 1920s. During the war, the consensus within the board on the
goals of schooling had been broken, and the board's relative independence from outside groups had been ended. Under pressure to
use the schools to help win a popular war, the board had allowed
the federal government and private groups into the schools. These
board actions were remembered after the war by fiscally and ideologically conservative groups who entered the school political arena.
The board not only did not regain its independence, but independence was no longer an important question as the board composition changed in the 1920s.

36. See Pendergrass, "Urban Reform and Voluntary Association: A Case Study of
the Seattle Municipal League, 1910–1929"; Saltvig, "The Progressive Movement in
Washington"; and Joan M. Jensen, *The Price of Vigilance* (Chicago: Rand McNally,
1968).

8

Postwar Patriotism and Progressive Education, 1919–1920

During World War I, outside groups used the Seattle schools to help win the war. The board may have viewed that as temporary, but after the war, patriotic and tax-cutting groups remembered these lessons well—the schools were vulnerable, they could be used as a ready-made propaganda network, and school politics could be engaged in by any organized group with a reasonable chance of success.

Three weeks after World War I had ended, the annual school and port elections occurred. Few people cared, with only 8,600 bothering to vote in a city of 313,500. People stayed home because of the serious influenza epidemic, because the war was over, and because these two minor elections with no compelling issues were easily ignored. In the preceding weeks, the newspapers had been filled with stories of postwar euphoria, but with hardly a paragraph about this school board election. The winning candidates in this almost unnoticed election, however, signaled two important themes in postwar school politics: continuing attempts to reduce expenditures, and a virtual abandonment of the board by socially prominent progressives.

The two 1918 winners were Henry B. King, who ran unopposed for George Spencer's seat, and Walter Santmyer, who defeated incumbent Evangeline C. Harper. King owned a men's clothing store and Santmyer was the chief steam and electrical engineer for Puget Sound Light and Traction Company. In a 1940 reminiscence, Board Secretary Reuben Jones characterized Santmyer as "a new and different type of man from the usual makeup of the board . . . being rather arbitrary, blunt and emphatic, and at times unique and force-

130

ful in his expressions."[1] Santmyer ran on the board's need for someone with his knowledge of building-construction practices. He charged that the heating plants at West Seattle High School and four or five grade schools were too costly. He appealed to voters wanting to save tax money, and he portrayed his building background as more useful on the board than that of a society club woman.

Walter Santmyer and Henry B. King were endorsed by the Central Labor Council. They were not from the ranks of labor, but labor perceived it best to have them elected, claiming it was not "an excuse to refrain from voting that one out of labor's ranks is not a candidate. When we cannot have the best we must strive for the next best, and not rest contented with allowing the reactionary forces to have everything their own way all the time."[2] But, once in office, the new board members hardly followed labor's platform.

At the first meeting of this new board, Socialist Richard Winsor was denied the board presidency, undoubtedly because of his opposition to the war. Board protocol for passing the presidency around by seniority was altered for the first time. Nathan Eckstein was elected instead.

In January 1919 King and Santmyer joined Ebenezer Shorrock in denying the use of the Broadway High School auditorium to the Socialists for a lecture by Max Eastman. Since 1911–1912, any group could use school facilities for meetings, and the Socialists had done so many times. But the new board members did not share that prewar, progressive spirit, which had considered schools as community facilities to be used "by the people." Further, the board decided "that for the time being, the use of school buildings be not granted for political or religious gatherings."[3] The board majority was concerned about labor unrest and trouble from radicals. The Central Labor Council, the Wobblies, and the Socialists were all tarred with the same brush and were labeled "radicals." And at the end of January, there was worrisome talk throughout Seattle about radicals shutting down the city with a strike.

1. Reuben Jones, Reminiscences, 1940, SP.
2. *Seattle Union Record*, December 7, 1918, p. 8.
3. Minutes of Board, January 31, 1919.

On Thursday, February 6, 1919, organized labor closed down most of Seattle with a General Strike. This General Strike grew out of shipyard workers' refusal to give up wage gains made during the war. Because war industry had been so important in Seattle, there was high postwar unemployment. Additionally, employers made ongoing attempts to cut wages. Shipyard workers went on strike, and the Seattle Central Labor Council became increasingly controlled by radicals who thought the time had come for direct action.[4]

The school board responded to the General Strike in ways that mirrored middle-class fears about radicals. But the board also had a special and symbolic interest in this strike—recalled board member Anna Louise Strong was a member of the General Strike Committee. Strong had written a crucial editorial in the *Seattle Union Record*, saying, "We are undertaking the most tremendous move ever made by LABOR in this country, a move which will lead—NO ONE KNOWS WHERE!"[5] That Strong was active in the General Strike seemed to vindicate the board and to give it an added incentive to keep schools open.

The board did not think teachers would walk off the job, but they were worried about the school engineers (boiler men and janitors), who belonged to AFL unions. The engineers had voted to strike. Then they had asked for an exemption from the General Strike Committee but had been refused. On the first morning of the strike, janitors did not report for work at most schools. The board that afternoon agreed to "engage caretakers for buildings where it may become necessary." The next day, Friday, only sixteen schools were open.

The board resolved to keep schools open, so it directed its chief engineer to order all engineers and janitors to be at work with their buildings open at the usual time Monday morning. The chief engineer was "authorized to fill the places of any janitors, engineers or firemen who failed to report for duty." At the open buildings, those who went to work were harassed. The board sent a statement to

4. See Robert L. Friedheim, *The Seattle General Strike* (Seattle: University of Washington Press, 1964).

5. *Seattle Union Record*, February 4, 1919, p. 1.

Mayor Ole Hanson asking him "to see that our principals, teachers, engineers, janitors and the children are afforded complete protection."[6] The strike ended on Tuesday, February 11, 1919, with labor and all political radicals in a worse position than before.

One month after the General Strike, and four months after the war had ended, the firing of "unpatriotic" teachers reached its final victim. The board asked for the resignation of Charles Neiderhauser, a popular history teacher at West Seattle High School. Neiderhauser was a Quaker who had registered for the draft as a conscientious objector. He was not drafted because he had a handicapped child. In addition to his convictions about war, he was the son-in-law of the Reverend Sydney Strong and the brother-in-law of Anna Louise Strong.[7] Neiderhauser was a popular teacher, and many West Seattle parents and students rallied to his defense. Supportive letters and petitions poured in to the board, including one from the High School Teachers' League. He also had strong support from Cooper.

The dismissal of Neiderhauser was tied in with two other issues: Cooper's promotion of the inquiry method of teaching high school history, and his advocacy of the Ginn series history textbooks. These issues increased the distance between Cooper and the lay board over Cooper's role as a professional educator. Cooper had promoted teaching techniques designed to make students think and reason, for example, the "project-problem method" in history. The war had had a corrosive effect on progressivism's tenets of learning as inquiry, and of education as teaching people how to think—as well as what to think about. Cooper's opposition to teaching-as-indoctrination was one of several incidents that hastened his retirement.

Cooper's defense of prewar pedagogy signaled his desire to get postwar schooling "back to normalcy"—to stop use of the classroom as an agency of wartime propaganda. Cooper defended high school history teachers by comparing American with German schooling:

6. Minutes of Board, February 6, 1919 (caretakers); ibid., February 7, 1919 (chief engineer authorized).

7. See Keith A. Murray, "The Charles Neiderhauser Case: Patriotism in the Seattle Schools, 1919," *Pacific Northwest Quarterly* 74, no. 1 (January 1983): 11–17.

There is an autocratic or Prussian method of instruction, and likewise a democratic or American method. In one case the government or external authority determines what the child shall know for the purposes of the government, and he is taught just that. The child asks no questions, and participates only as he memorizes what is handed out to him by the state-instructed teacher. In the other case, what the child should know is determined by his capacity and willingness to learn, to discriminate, and to reason. He is permitted and encouraged to ask questions, to investigate, to discuss and to rationalize.

Cooper argued that students of history, civics, and economics must learn of competing ideas and must discuss in class the differing views on a question. The teacher was to be a guide and was to make no "attempt either directly or indirectly to mould the minds of his pupils to his particular way of thinking. . . . Propagandism of any kind in a school is not only inadmissible, but intolerable."[8]

In the context of wartime propaganda in the schools, with six teachers already fired and Neiderhauser under investigation, Cooper's defense of prewar pedagogy was courageous. He boldly asserted that "every teacher should be permitted to think and act for himself, upon political and economic questions, and he should not be called to account for his political views or for voting in accordance with them."[9] But the school board was interested in a narrower view of patriotism than was Cooper.

The board asked Cooper to report on the methods used to teach history, especially classroom discussion. Cooper gave his report both to defend Neiderhauser and to defend prewar progressive pedagogy to a board suspicious of both—and no longer sure about him. Cooper steadfastly supported not only the discussion methods he had previously worked to instill but also the teachers who taught that way. He claimed that instruction in the social sciences in Seattle "corresponds to that which obtains generally in the secondary schools throughout the United States." Indeed, "most of our sol-

8. Frank Cooper, Memorandum to School Board, February 28, 1919, SP, Folder "Methods in Instruction."
9. Ibid.

diers and sailors under thirty years of age who have had a high school education have been taught by that method." Although high school students are "not mature in judgment," they should be taught through discussion methods "in order that they may be trained in the processes of thinking." The method used "aims to blaze the way to just conclusions, rather than to arrive at conclusions, for there are numerous problems studied as to which satisfactory conclusions have not yet been reached."[10]

In closing, Cooper asked the board to protect teachers like Neiderhauser "for the sake of a great institution and of the children of the people." These are, said Cooper, "trying times for teachers," because "they are censored in a most critical way by both the well-meaning and the malicious, and they live and work in an atmosphere which is hard for them and bad for the schools." Teachers, declared Cooper, need sympathy and they need protection.[11]

The board was neither sympathetic nor protective. It fired Charles Neiderhauser on March 7, 1919. Only Richard Winsor voted to retain Neiderhauser, thundering, "I must have facts and not unsupported assertions coming to me from such sources as the complaints against this teacher." Winsor delivered to the board a blistering, rambling statement condemning the arrogance of the rich and powerful, who maintained themselves at the expense of workers by suppressing fundamental rights. He fumed, "I pray God that the time will never come when the right of free speech and a free press, and a discussion of what is righteous and just, will be suppressed by the lick-spittle journals of the great moneyed interests." Secretary James Duncan of the Central Labor Council said in disgust that the board "has been one of the most spineless, jellyfish school boards that ever existed. The board permitted the discharging of Charles Neiderhauser because Neiderhauser permitted his pupils to think for themselves."[12]

Cooper's support of Neiderhauser and of progressive methods to

10. Frank Cooper, Memorandum to School Board, March 6, 1919, SP, Folder "Methods in Instruction."
11. Ibid.
12. Minutes of Board, March 7, 1919 (Winsor); *Seattle Union Record*, December 2, 1919, p. 2 (Duncan).

135

teach history was consistent with his support of the Ginn series of world history textbooks. The series was reissued in the winter of 1919, but because of continued objections to the authors, the board refused again to buy these textbooks. Further, the board rescinded its August 15, 1917, adoption of the Ginn textbooks. After citing the suspect activities of authors Charles Beard and James Robinson, board members said they no longer felt that

> it comes within their duty to stand sponsor for or to defend the use of textbooks on history whose authors have been subjected to charges that, in the present state of public feeling, give offense to many citizens and patrons of the public schools, nor believe that it is wise to cause the schools to bear the burden of contention and criticism sure to follow upon the attempted use of histories known to be written by the authors mentioned.[13]

The views of the Seattle Minute Men, in the context of the war and the General Strike, had prevailed over those of the superintendent, the principals, and the history teachers. The board no longer listened uncritically to Cooper as its expert, but now viewed him as one competing voice among several—including outsiders. To the board it seemed folly to buy a textbook not only tainted by "unpatriotic" authors and a pro-German bias, but removed by the publisher for revision. Further, it seemed dangerous to leave tainted teachers in the classroom, encouraged by the superintendent to hold discussions with students about controversial issues. In the context of Strong's recall, the General Strike, and the strength of the Minute Men, the new board voted its perception of public opinion. It would not be the last time the board opposed Cooper's judgment. For years Cooper had deferred to the board on bricks-and-mortar questions, and they to him on matters of personnel, curriculum, and pedagogy. Now the de facto division of power had been challenged, and the board had entered the educator's domain.

Cooper's influence was further reduced by a reorganization of the administration in the spring of 1919. Cooper had written a long

13. Minutes of Board, March 7, 1919.

memorandum to board member Ebenezer Shorrock, making it quite clear that the superintendent should be the chief executive officer of the board, and that the heads of the various departments should be subordinate to the superintendent. Instead, the board had proceeded to decentralize administration into six separate departments; namely, education (superintendent), business (board secretary), supplies, architecture, maintenance and repairs, and medical. Cooper was not pleased. Shorrock also opposed this reorganization, "because experience in our own District has shown the desirability of centralization . . . and because in most of the large cities of the country it has been found best to have not more than two executives, whereas the plan now adopted virtually creates five."[14]

For the December 1919 school board election, the only issue was patriotism. Walter Santmyer was now running for a full term, and attorney George H. Walker was running to replace retiring Nathan Eckstein. They were opposed by candidates of the Triple Alliance, a coalition of farmers (the Grange), independent railroad unions, and the Washington Federation of Labor. Walker, Santmyer, and the newspapers saw the election in terms of patriotism rather than school issues. The *Seattle Times* was blunt, calling this election "the fight for unadulterated Americanism." The Bolo Club, an organization of Spanish-American and World War I veterans, appealed for five hundred cars to take voters to the polls. "Automobile owners," they said, "you can help the fight for Americanism."[15]

George H. Walker linked his Triple Alliance opponents to the radicals who controlled the Central Labor Council and led the General Strike: "The identical crew that proclaimed the revolution of February 4, though now under a different standard, proposes to enter the citadel on December 2. It should not be permitted." At their closing election rally, Walker and Santmyer said they would "keep out of her educational system any taint of Bolshevism, I.W.W. syndicalism, Soviet rule or any other un-American issue." Additionally, both promised to get rid of unpatriotic teachers. Santmyer alleged

14. Frank Cooper, Memorandum to Ebenezer Shorrock, February 4, 1921, SP, Folder "Organization"; Board Report, April 11, 1919, SP, Folder "Organization" (Shorrock).

15. *Seattle Times*, November 29, 1919, p. 1; ibid., December 1, 1919, p. 1.

that "more than 90 percent of all teachers in the Seattle Schools were 100 percent American and were teaching American ideals and principles."[16]

Walker's speeches demonstrated how far this election had strayed from school curricular or bricks-and-mortar issues. Walker charged that, because of the General Strike, Seattle was now known nationally as the "home of the Bolsheviki." Walker wanted to send the nation a message that the majority in Seattle were loyal Americans. "Let us roll up a two- or three-to-one vote for Americanism and rule by the majority," he urged.[17] Nobody said much about schools.

Had anyone been listening to the Triple Alliance candidates, they would have heard two important dissenting themes. The Triple Alliance was unhappy with the current centrally directed, hierarchical approach to schooling. It wanted teachers to have more control over their teaching, with a reduced role for supervisors. Its candidates advocated "a larger participation of the teachers in determining educational policies." Second, the Triple Alliance affirmed its belief "in an educational system directed by educators instead of by the business interests." They stated: "We believe that the highest duty of the teacher is to teach the pupils to think independently, and we denounce as a crime against our children any attempt to intimidate teachers or pupils in the exercise of free discussion."[18] This last was also a reference to the firing of teachers, especially Charles Neiderhauser.

With a large voter turnout, George H. Walker and Walter Santmyer easily won—about 27,000 to 18,000. School elections have not often been plebiscites on Americanism, but this 1919 election certainly took on that appearance. Walker resigned after one year, confessing that he had run only to prevent a Triple Alliance candidate from winning. "I was urged to help make the fight in opposition," he said, "and reluctantly and only under the emergency of the situation became a candidate for the School Board. That emergency has passed, and in the face of the imperative demands of my

16. Ibid., November 29, 1919, p. 1 (Walker); ibid., December 1, 1919, p. 1 (closing rally); ibid., December 2, 1919, p. 1 (Santmyer).

17. Ibid., December 2, 1919, p. 1.

18. *Seattle Union Record*, December 1, 1919, p. 3.

own work I am asking to be relieved."[19] Those were hardly the reasons prewar progressives had run for the board.

Immediately after the 1919 election, an old issue resurfaced—whether teachers could hold a second job. The issue came to the board because of postwar inflation and the desire by some teachers to work during Christmas vacations. Walter Santmyer was an outspoken advocate of letting teachers hold two jobs. Santmyer said in his reelection platform that "teachers at all times should be free to do as they see fit in the hours that they are not at work for the school district. . . . A teacher who does nothing but teach and go home and lives in that kind of an environment cannot have as broad a view as if she were allowed to enter into other vocations than that of teaching, during her leisure hours."[20]

The issue of second jobs for teachers had a long history. For years the board had prohibited teachers from holding a second job during the school year, although they could teach night school or work in the summer. The rule read: "No principal, teacher, janitor or other regular employee of the district shall engage in any occupation that will interfere with his or her duties as such employee." In 1916 Cooper claimed that this rule "appears to cover completely the interests of the district without imposing restrictions which might imperil good feeling and call for frequent acts of legislation." Further, he said there had been few violations of this rule over the years.[21] Teachers occasionally asked for and received board permission to hold a second job.

As inflation worsened during and after the war, and as irritation increased between teachers and the board over salary, the board prohibited teachers from working during vacations. In the fall and winter of 1919–1920, Cooper sided with the teachers who wanted to end restrictions on vacation work. "Teachers are made to feel by being prohibited that they are unduly restricted in their freedom," he argued, and that this restriction "is a reflection upon their wis-

19. Minutes of Board, January 21, 1921.
20. *Seattle Times*, December 1, 1919, p. 2.
21. Frank Cooper, Memorandum to School Board, August 7, 1916, SP, Folder "Outside Employment of Teachers"; ibid., December 8, 1919, SP, Folder "Outside Employment of Teachers" (few violations).

dom and professional spirit." He thought this perception was widespread among teachers, and that "its effect upon the good will and working spirit of the corps at large [was] bad."[22] Cooper noted that in these postwar years the board annually allowed about one hundred day-school teachers to teach in evening school, which was detrimental to their daytime teaching. It would have been better, he felt, to prohibit day teachers from teaching night school, letting them teach summer school instead, which was currently forbidden.

Cooper also wondered if the board intended to stop those teachers who supplemented their income by selling produce from their gardens, or by raising and selling a few chickens, or by writing articles for newspapers or magazines. Cooper concluded: "I believe the schools will not suffer but benefit by an abrogation of the rule."[23] At the meeting of December 12, 1919, the new board decided to suspend the prohibition for the upcoming Christmas vacation only. But the board was neither moved nor amused by Cooper's image of teachers as chicken farmers, and the prohibition on outside work took effect again after Christmas 1919.

In the spring of 1920, the board's attitude toward organized labor changed from suspicious to hostile. Throughout the country, labor was fighting the open-shop movement. In Seattle, the board started purposefully to spend its public money on nonunion contractors. In April the American Association of Craftsmen and Workmen asked that any contract let by the board be open to nonunion employers. The board then decided to put a clause in all future contracts that the work "is to be open to any American citizen."[24] Previously the board had declined to put an open- or closed-shop clause in contracts. Leaving the issue unresolved had, in practice, resulted in a fair amount of union business.

In subsequent days, the board defined that clause in terms actively hostile to organized labor. The board amended the clause to say that the district would take over a contractor's work if he did the work "on the principle of what is commonly known as the 'closed

22. Ibid., December 8, 1919, SP, Folder "Outside Employment of Teachers."
23. Ibid.
24. Minutes of Board, April 30, 1920.

shop,' or if the services of American citizens, being competent workmen, are refused by the contractor upon the ground or for the reason that such workmen are not members of a workman's organization, or of some particular organization."[25] Richard Winsor voted
against this antiunion clause. In countless similar ways, the General
Strike contributed to the postwar, antiunion sentiment of managers
and businessmen.

In the spring of 1920, the board gave teachers a small salary increase for the school year 1920–1921. They also sent a memorandum
to the state legislature urging appointment of a special commission
to study how best to finance schools. Seattle was in an economic recession, unemployment was high, and governmental agencies were
trying to lower taxes. While the chamber of commerce commended
the schools for giving only a small salary increase, the principals and
high school teachers complained. The High School Men Teachers'
Club even asked if married men could "be given an extra period of
service, with proportionate increased pay."[26]

As summer 1920 approached, teachers upset with a miserly pay
raise flooded the board with requests for permission to work during
the summer. At the June 11 board meeting, Board President Richard
Winsor gave permission to Assistant Superintendent Thomas Cole
to teach summer school at the University of Washington, although
he denied all teacher requests for permission to work. Winsor refused to admit that teachers needed more money, "when we are
paying or are about to pay, liberal salaries." The Socialist Winsor
spoke for all when he said a teacher holding a vacation job would be
"thereby taking the bread out of the mouths of many persons who
have to seek employment for a living and are unable to obtain positions on account of their being filled by those to whom the school
district is paying at least a fair salary."[27] To admit that salaries were
so low that teachers needed a second job would put the board under
more pressure to raise salaries at a time when tax-cutting groups
wanted salaries reduced.

After the board reaffirmed its prohibition on outside work, thirty-

25. Ibid., May 7, 1920.
26. Ibid., March 19, 1920 (commission); ibid., May 7, 1920 (high school men).
27. Ibid., June 11, 1920.

three teachers, in an unheard of demonstration of frustration, attached protests to their contracts about this rule. The board responded to this teacher impudence by declaring that these contracts were not a satisfactory response. It gave the thirty-three teachers until June 15 to turn their contracts in without protest, or be dropped. Two declined, and thirty-one turned them in, although they attached "a separate communication still disapproving the restriction in regard to outside work."[28]

This incident is reflective not only of poor morale among some teachers but also of the way relationships between the board and teachers had changed. This action was not taken by a formal teachers' group, but by teachers acting on their own in response to an immediate problem. At a moment when organized labor was weakening in Seattle, and when the board was awarding construction contracts only to open-shop contractors, a small group of teachers was exhibiting the ingredients for a teachers' union. Charles B. Stillman, president of the American Federation of Teachers, had been in Seattle in November 1919 and had talked to the teachers.

It was inevitable that Seattle teachers would think of organizing themselves into one association or union, as was occurring in many cities.[29] For some Seattle teachers, organizing was especially appealing in the context of bitter struggles with the board during and right after World War I. The issues of salary, firing of teachers suspected of disloyalty, and the right to work during vacations were the kinds of issues to cause some teachers, especially the high school teachers, to think of themselves as "labor" and the board as "management."

A teachers' association or union was not formed in Seattle for several reasons: the board was opposed; Cooper had a moderating influence as the teachers' advocate to the board; and teachers were reluctant to identify themselves with the Seattle labor movement because of its radical tendencies and leaders. Seattle teachers kept allegiance to small subgroups of teachers rather than to one group analogous to "labor." They also chose to be poor and dependent, but respectable in the eyes of middle-class parents.

28. Ibid., June 18, 1920.
29. See Urban, *Why Teachers Organized*.

142

In a national sense, teacher unions in these decades had limited success getting and staying organized. Teachers had no national organization, since the National Education Association (NEA) was for administrators, principals, university professors, and college presidents. The NEA was mostly male, while most public school teachers were female. The most prominent teachers' union, the Chicago Teachers' Federation, had lost much of its influence after the Chicago school board had fired forty key union members in 1917.

Because grade and high school teachers thought of themselves as quite different groups, Seattle teachers did not form even one umbrella teachers' organization, not to mention a union. While some high school teachers were leading the fight for higher salaries and turning in their contracts with protest messages on them, the grade school women were publicly quiet. Unmarried and always underpaid—and without property, family, or financial security—they were unlikely to take chances. When board member Henry B. King resigned, they sent him a letter expressing "our appreciation to you for your unfailing courtesy, for your sympathy with our cause and for the able and efficient manner in which you have handled all matters pertaining to the Seattle schools."[30] This was hardly the stuff of incipient unionism.

Seattle teachers thought of themselves as respectable white-collar professionals, an image at odds with the Seattle area union movement. Seattle unionism was characterized by a radical wing, links to Socialists, attempts to elect union members to political office, and suspect patriotism. Especially after the federal government crackdown on Wobblies under the Espionage Act, and after the General Strike, the Seattle labor movement was tainted as un-American, radical, and revolutionary. For teachers to respond to unions, they first had to think of themselves in terms of labor versus management. Instead, teachers identified themselves with their managers, especially with their chief advocate Superintendent Cooper.

The board, however, thought of teachers as labor and of itself as management. The board perceived its task as keeping labor costs down and labor unorganized. It did not like teachers allied with

30. Minutes of Board, January 13, 1922.

those of "dissimilar occupations." Dissimilar occupations would result in "the usual turmoil that generally follows differences of opinion in labor disputes such as the lockout, picket system, debarment of nonunion workers, the boycott and the enforcement of claims by resort to politics."[31]

Cooper was hardly an advocate of teacher unionism, preferring to be seen as the teachers' advocate to the board. Cooper reported favorably on a speech on "Teacher Organization" he had heard at the 1920 NEA meeting. The speech, by Lotus Delta Coffman of the University of Minnesota, "advocated the formation of professional organizations and the use of such organizations in promoting higher standards and better conditions, but opposed alliance by teachers with any other class or group." Cooper quoted Coffman as saying: "If democracy is to be made safe, the teachers of our future citizens must be able to remain free from class prejudice as professional public servants, must see the prejudice to any class, and labor to dispel the ignorance and cultivate the unselfishness which makes class disputes impossible."[32] A progressive like Cooper was uncomfortable in a situation where the teachers would view him as their adversary because they were "labor" and he was "management."

The December 1920 board election was notable because Richard Winsor, the eighty-four-year-old Socialist, was defeated for reelection. His nine years of being the conscience of the board were used against him by opponents touting fiscal economy and patriotism. Fundamentally, Winsor was attacked because, as a Socialist, he had helped shape the prewar school system, and he had not given the war effort 100 percent. The *Seattle Union Record* reported that Winsor's challenger, Carl Croson, "declared for Americanism without defining it and said he represented certain classes in the fight for a place on the board." Such code words—"Americanism" and "class"—constituted the attack on Winsor. Additionally, Winsor's age and health were used against him, despite the fact that in the preceding two years he had held the second best attendance record at board meetings, missing only 14 of 150 meetings. Winsor fought

31. School board statement, undated, SP, Folder "Teacher Unions."
32. Frank Cooper, Memorandum to School Board, February 28, 1920, SP, Folder "Vacations."

back vigorously, charging that the *Seattle Times* and *Seattle Post Intelligencer* "daily spread more filth than 100 school systems could eradicate." The ability of the school system, he said, was "taxed to its utmost to offset this filth."[33]

Richard Winsor narrowly lost. Out of about 30,000 votes, Winsor was defeated by about 2,500, suggesting good support for his positions. The postwar change in the mood of the voter was hardly overwhelming. Neither Anna Louise Strong during the war nor Richard Winsor after the war was decisively repudiated. As Winsor departed, his colleagues praised him, but Henry B. King undoubtedly spoke for others when he noted that Winsor often made him "powerfully mad." In Winsor's farewell remarks to the board, he noted that much of his life

> has been in opposition to the making of human beings, either in part or in whole, by any power, economic or otherwise, human slaves. This may be deemed radicalism. I don't care what you call it—it is the type of American citizenship for which I hope and towards which my efforts have been directed upon this board.[34]

Immediately after Winsor's defeat, Ebenezer Shorrock moved that school elections be held with the nonpartisan municipal elections in May of each year. The measure passed, with Winsor and King opposed. The new postwar board wanted to ensure a large enough voter turnout so that Socialists, labor, or any "radical" group would not be likely to elect a member. The national red scare had convinced many that revolution was entirely possible. The examples of anarchist bombings, the Boston police strike, and the deportations of radical aliens gave local radical events added portent. Political leaders everywhere worked to make sure that radicals could not take political power. The Seattle school board was no exception—hence the shift of board elections to the municipal election. By the first combined election in 1922, Frank Cooper had resigned, Richard Winsor was gone, and a new type of board member and superintendent were taking power.

33. *Seattle Union Record*, December 3, 1920, p. 1.
34. Minutes of Board, December 10, 1920 (Henry King); ibid., December 31, 1920 (Winsor).

9

Doing Less with Less,
1920–1922

In the early 1920s citizen tax-cutting groups attempted to gain control of the Seattle school board. The goal of these fiscally and ideologically conservative groups was to cut taxes, both by dismantling the schools' social welfare programs and by offering a reduced curriculum, mostly of basic academic classes. Their vision of urban schooling was that of a school system offering far less than it had ever offered under Superintendent Cooper. Cooper was driven to resign, and the system he had built was modified. It is well to remember, however, that this was not a massive civic crusade against the schools. Only a handful of voters participated in this change, and they still passed bond issues each year. Essentially, these highly organized, influential groups helped elect several candidates, tipping the board's balance. Cooper was vulnerable and unable to ward off their pressure.

The most prominent critic within the system became Ebenezer Shorrock, a banker and member of the board since 1902. Shorrock had always been the board's specialist in financial matters. During and after the war, he became much more fiscally conservative. He advocated reducing expenses by cutting salaries, but retaining the programs and services of the progressive era system he had helped build.

The postwar critics of governmental taxing and spending levels formed into three main groups. The original group, the Voters Information League (VIL), was organized in January 1921. Because of its success, a coalition of fifty civic groups interested in cutting taxes formed the Tax Reduction Council (TRC). The third group was the chamber of commerce's Bureau of Taxation, with which Ebenezer

Shorrock was closely allied. All agreed that wartime wages were artificially high and had to be lowered. In the private sector, they believed that labor unions would either have to agree to reduce wages or be broken by an open-shop movement. In the public sector, they believed taxation levels had to be reduced. The TRC claimed that "decreased cost of government is the most urgent problem before the country today. . . . We have found high taxes to mean loose methods and extravagant management, incompetent planning and wasteful execution. The penalty for a continuation of this is BANK-RUPTCY. Eternal vigilance is the price of liberty, and our liberty is bound up with taxation."[1]

After the 1920 school board election, the board majority walked hand in glove with the tax-cutting groups. When the chamber of commerce president urged "greater economy on the part of all public bodies," the board promptly passed a resolution stating its readiness "to cooperate by seeing that the schools are conducted with the expenditure of the least possible amount of money." After the VIL president addressed the board on "retrenchment," the board responded that "this question [was] now receiving their full attention and that the matters to which they referred would be given due consideration." Regarding the TRC, the board agreed "to cooperate with them in every way possible."[2] Cooper must have been deeply hurt by the realization that the board was closer to the tax-cutting forces than to him, especially when the TRC engaged him in a pamphlet war in 1921–1922.

At issue between Cooper and the TRC were the curriculum, teacher salaries, social welfare services, and control of the school system. The TRC wanted a curriculum with core liberal arts classes, and without the practical and vocational classes. They wanted teacher salaries cut, and social welfare services shifted to other agencies. And they advocated strong lay control over the hierarchical administration the educational experts had created. In urging these changes, they attacked Cooper personally, calling for a new superintendent who was younger and without vested ties.

1. Tax Reduction Council, Report on Seattle Public School's Medical Department, 1921, SP, Folder "Tax Reduction Council."
2. Minutes of Board, June 24, 1921.

The TRC clearly wanted high schools to get "back to the basics" and improve the "product" in academic subjects. They shared the traditional conservative understanding of schools as providers of excellent academic instruction, with low overhead and no "fads " or "frills." They complained that "the schools are now running, in addition to the regular academic courses, business colleges, shops, art and music conservatories, and now if the public wishes the addition of dramatic departments, it is possible to have them."[3]

The TRC also wanted to cut back extracurricular activities. They felt that such activities took their toll both on student schoolwork and on faculty health, morale, and quality of teaching. The TRC viewed the extracurriculum as the principal's "means of making himself popular with the pupils and possibly with the neighborhood." The TRC charged that, with school activities, students did not care as much about scholarship as before. Complained the TRC: "It is an enviable honor to belong to an athletic team, to the stage force, to take part in a show, but no one envies or even notices the few students on the honor roll for excellent scholarship. That is so very old-fashioned and humdrum."[4] The TRC recommended that these outside activities be cut, thereby enabling the principal to do his main job without a vice-principal, clerks, and boys' and girls' advisors.

The systematic attack on Frank Cooper from ideological conservatives can probably be best summarized by a letter to the board from Mrs. George A. Smith. Mrs. Smith was prominent in club work and the women's suffrage movement, having served as president of the Washington Equal Suffrage Association in 1909. In the 1920s she was active in the TRC as chair of its high school committee. Mrs. Smith saw herself working with other conservatives around the country to reform schooling. "The American people as a nation," she claimed, "are endeavoring to save civilization from destruction by a return to the former American principles of honor, integrity, thrift and

3. Report of Survey of Executive Staff of Seattle Public Schools, June 28, 1921, p. 15, SP, Folder "Tax Reduction Council."
4. Ibid., p. 16, SP, Folder "Tax Reduction Council."

duty."[5] She shared an unease with her peers over the way the city of Seattle was changing. Socialist agitation in the streets, labor strife and strikes, Wobblies, the need to recall a school board member, inflation, recession, and the General Strike were all sobering events for affluent conservatives. They felt that somehow the schools must instill bedrock American values in young people to counter the influence of tumultuous changes.

Mrs. Smith postulated seven causes of the "breakdown" of the school system, each of which she attributed to Frank Cooper. "Breakdown" was the wrong image, since prior to Cooper there had not been much of a school system in Seattle. There was no past "Golden Age" in Seattle to cite for reference. Her concerns, then, were really aimed at Seattle's current life. They reflected the strains of a port town that had rapidly become a medium-sized city.

Mrs. Smith asserted that schools trained the memory ("a very evident poll-parrot repetition and monkey imitation") without teaching students to think and reason. Her comment, in fact, described the pedagogical result of the shift to large schools and mass education. As noted earlier, however, Cooper had consistently advocated (with mixed results) teaching students to think rather than recite. Second, she did not like the "so-called development of the individuality of the child, which is in reality laziness and cowardice on the part of the teachers." Third, she argued that the extracurriculum built up a "social caste, with all its diabolical intricacies, which are absolutely foreign to a democratic form of government. . . . I hold these activities responsible for the greater part of the moral and spiritual deterioration of our youth."

Mrs. Smith also objected to nonintellectual classes, such as manual training and domestic science. Such classes did not teach people to think, nor did they inculcate the ideals of the society. Instead, they kept people repressed, ignorant, and victimized: "The autocratic ages long ago discovered that the mind engaged in making fudge, embroidering posies on a piece of cloth, making raffia mats

5. Mrs. George A. Smith, Memorandum to School Board, March 21, 1922, SP, Folder "Tax Reduction Council."

and bird houses, cannot at the same time engage in an analysis of the meaning of the Declaration of Independence, nor a contemplation of the tyrannies of empires and kingdoms in comparison with the liberties and happiness of an American Republic."

Mrs. Smith charged, in addition, that "supervised study" made pupils lazy, lowered the standards of scholarship, led to easier courses of study, and discouraged and demoralized teachers. As a sixth point, she was not amused by the Parent-Teacher Association, which she described as part of Cooper's political machine. And seventh, she objected to textbooks that were "compiled with the view of imparting information to inferior minds rather than training the minds to reason and retain."

Mrs. Smith concluded her attack against Cooper and other progressive era educators ("The problem is national and not local.") by trumpeting lay control: "The American people have allowed the paid educators to dictate the policies of our educational system, with an absolute contempt for the judgment and intelligence of the parents of this country, and they have succeeded so well in throttling the protests of their opponents that they are planning an even more complete and total enslavement through the process of initiative and legislative laws."

Mrs. Smith's report, along with reports from other ideologically conservative critics, outlined a desire not to return schooling to the prewar level, but to reduce schooling to a minimal level that had never existed under Cooper. Schooling in Seattle since 1901–1902 had incorporated aspects of social welfare and service. It had not been solely an academic system for only those students who were doing well in school on their own. As schooling became a large systematic enterprise, Cooper and the board saw their roles as doing whatever was necessary to persuade children and youth in school to improve their health, knowledge, and citizenship. The conservative critics had an alternate vision—urban schooling would offer a core of academic classes, and that was all. Those students who could attend, stay, and appreciate such an experience were to do so. Others were to leave school and do other things—which was not the business of the state through an agency like the schools.

The first successful legal challenge to the Seattle progressives' understanding of schooling came in January 1921, when a Washington Supreme Court ruling closed the school clinic. The court ruled that the district had no legal basis to operate a medical and dental clinic. The state legislature in 1909 had given districts the right to appoint a medical inspector to decide "all questions of sanitation and health affecting the safety and welfare of the public schools" and to inspect schools. Now the court ruled that what Dr. Brown was supervising in Seattle was "more properly designated as a 'hospital' " and must be stopped, except for the parental schools.[6] While the tax-cutting groups were not part of this suit, it was consistent with their agenda. The district's right to operate a school clinic was successfully challenged by a group of parents. At issue were vaccination, hygiene instruction, and compulsory physical examinations.

During the war, the loopholes for a student to avoid the compulsory physical education class had been eliminated. A requirement before starting this class was a physical and dental examination. The board was concerned about legal liability in case of an accident. In May 1919 a parent objected to these examinations, saying that "the home, and not the school, will look after the child's health." Cooper asked the board if, in such cases, "we shall be equally insistent that the children shall have immediate attention, and whether we would be warranted in excluding children persisting in the attitude of nonconformance." The board decided to hold firm on physical and dental examinations. A parent then appealed unsuccessfully to the board and to the county superintendent.[7]

This dispute was widened when two children were suspended from Lafayette School because they had refused to have a dental examination. Dr. Brown reported to the board that no exemptions were granted, and this included the dental examinations. A list was then presented to the board of all children excluded from school because they would not undergo examinations. Board attorney H. W.

6. "A school district has no authority to render free medical services to pupils by maintaining a clinic for the treatment of school children of parents unable to pay for regular professional services" (*Session Laws* 1909, Section 16, p. 239). See also *McGilvra* v. *Seattle School District No. 1*, 113 Wash., January 1921.

7. Frank Cooper, Memorandum to School Board, July 2, 1919, SP, Folder "Medical Department"; Minutes of Board, October 24, 1919; ibid., November 21, 1919 (appeal).

Pennock supported the suspensions by giving an opinion that children must either be examined and attend, or must go to a private school. Failing these, the attendance officer should file a complaint with a judge. The board subsequently received five petitions for exemptions from medical examinations, "numberously signed." The parents appealed this decision to the county superintendent, who ruled in favor of the district. The parents appealed to the State Superintendent of Public Instruction, who upheld the board and the county superintendent.[8]

In addition to physical and dental examinations, some parents opposed the medical department because of Dr. Brown's support for sex and health education. Dr. Brown believed strongly that children should not be kept in ignorance about "sex hygiene." He advocated sex education for all grades, starting in the first grade with "plant life and then the butterfly" and gradually reaching humans. "There would be no shock incident to such instruction," he confidently asserted. A parent protested against "talks [to students] on Hygiene, and also how to take care of themselves from a medical standpoint," and concluded, "we do not wish to have [our daughter] listen to these talks as we consider them not necessary and would like to have her excused from them." Board attorney Pennock said the study of hygiene was compulsory, citing "four sections of the law."[9]

Still other parents opposed Dr. Brown and the medical department for its support of smallpox vaccination. These parents formed the Public Schools Protective League, which led the attack on the school medical department. In late March 1919 smallpox appeared at West Seattle High School and the nearby Lafayette School. The board ordered that in any school exposed to smallpox, the "School Medical Inspector shall require presentation of a certificate of vaccination as a condition of school membership and admittance to the school." Shortly after, "a large delegation" protested the policy at

8. Minutes of Board, December 12, 1919 (dental examinations); ibid., March 5, 1920 (county superintendent); ibid., July 2, 1920 (state superintendent).

9. *Annual Report*, 1913–1914, p. 73 (Brown); Frank Cooper, Memorandum to School Board, July 2, 1919, SP, Folder "Medical Department" (parent); Minutes of Board, January 30, 1920 (Pennock).

the April 4 board meeting. The board passed responsibility to the Seattle Commissioner of Health "and referred the petitioners to that authority, who alone could grant relief."[10] The vaccination opponents were not fooled. On April 25, 1919, they sued Brown and the board.

After the state supreme court ordered the medical clinic closed, the board asked attorney Pennock to determine what part of the medical department could continue, and to draft a bill for the next session of the legislature. The board resolved "that the work should be continued, and that it [would] do all in its power through a committee or otherwise, to get legislative authority for carrying on the work as heretofore." Two weeks later it reopened the clinic, now paid for by the city Department of Health and Sanitation, but with Brown still on the school payroll. In the spring, the Red Cross took over the clinic and ran it for the schools. Cooper did not like the fact that the schools were now closely allied to an outside organization. Echoing a prewar board position, he said, "I very much doubt the wisdom of making the public schools, even for the purpose of serving noble ends, an instrument for the promotion or fostering of the interests of an outside organization, chiefly because the schools should be kept as free of entanglement as possible."[11]

In the spring of 1921 the board started making its first cutbacks. Nonteaching salaries were cut (e.g., carpenters, painters, janitors, and engineers); the school garden program was dropped; and elementary manual training and domestic science were dropped. A substantial protest against these cuts quickly came from various PTA and community groups; indeed, they often urged that the garden, manual training, and domestic science programs not only be reinstated, but expanded. All were classes in which children learned through activity rather than seatwork, and all were good examples of progressive pedagogy. A year later, the Federation of Women's Clubs was still asking that elementary domestic science be resumed. The board replied to one such petition, citing "the difficulty con-

10. Minutes of Board, March 25, 1919 (smallpox); ibid., April 4, 1919 (refer to city commissioner).

11. Ibid., January 7, 1921; Frank Cooper, Memorandum to School Board, April 1, 1921, SP, Folder "Junior Red Cross."

153

fronting it in attempts to comply with the demand from many quarters for a reduction in the tax rate on the one hand, and from those who object to the curtailment of any educational activity on the other."[12]

The cuts continued in preparation for the fall of 1921. The board asked Cooper where further cuts could be made. He reluctantly suggested "pruning here and there," although he refused to recommend specific cuts. "The change suggested will be a backward step," he warned, "and the progress of the schools will be retarded." The board decided to hire no new teachers for 1921–1922 and, for the first time ever, to lay off some teachers.[13] Ebenezer Shorrock dissented, wanting to reduce salaries rather than personnel and programs.

The TRC issued a major report on June 28, 1921, sharply critical of Cooper's performance and of the size of the superintendent's office. To help run a district of over 40,000 students, Cooper had three assistant superintendents, one clerk, and seven stenographers. The TRC wanted to replace Cooper with a "young, virile Superintendent," reduce the assistant superintendents to one, and reduce the number of stenographers. All of the administrators were perceived as Cooper's "strong political clique . . . willing to carry forward the many costly frills that have been inaugurated in the past five years."[14]

The TRC repeated this theme in criticizing Cooper: a younger man who was an outsider to the district was needed as superintendent. They observed that "some able young educator who could take hold of our schools, free from all entangling alliances, should be chosen to inaugurate a system far less expensive, without materially reducing the efficiency of our schools." They wanted Cooper fired because they did not believe he could or would cut costs. Chiding the board for not yet making deep cuts, they asked: "Have you any idea

12. Minutes of Board, April 15, 1921 (school garden); ibid., May 6, 1921 (elementary manual training and domestic science).

13. Frank Cooper, Memorandum to School Board, May 20, 1921, SP, Folder "Expenditures"; Minutes of Board, May 24, 1921 (teacher layoffs).

14. Tax Reduction Council, Memorandum to School Board, August 1921, SP, Folder "Tax Reduction Council."

you can do this, or come anywhere near doing it, with Mr. Cooper and his Assistants in control of our schools?" In an undated letter to the board, the Voters Information League claimed that "Superinten dent Cooper has resisted every suggestion looking toward lessening school costs. He seems to be proud of the single fact that he has inaugurated and maintains the most costly system of public school education in the United States. . . . If any city ever needed a business educator at the head of its schools, this city does right now."[15]

Saving tax money was the point of attacking the size of administration, but closely tied was a conservative backlash against the modern institutional hierarchy of "professionals." The backlash was not against teachers, but against nonteaching administrators. The number of students had grown from 10,017 in 1901 to 42,241 in 1922. Consequently, the number of central office administrators had increased. Late in his tenure, Cooper had tried unsuccessfully to establish a hierarchical bureaucracy similar to the corporate model followed by other leading school administrators. Unlike many cities, however, Seattle actually had very few central office people.

Cooper supervised six directors of the Departments of Method, Home Economics, Music, Drawing and Design, Manual Training, and Physical Training. He had charge of eight supervisors and sixteen assistants who spent their days in the schools. "Be it remembered," the TRC noted, "none of these people teach; their sole business is supervision of teachers." The TRC wanted to replace these with a single supervisor of each department. Further, the TRC wanted eliminated the chairman of each department in each high school, to be replaced by one person who taught part-time and looked after the needs of that subject part-time.[16]

15. Ibid.; see also Voters Information League, Memorandum to School Board, undated, SP, Folder "Tax Reduction Council."

16. Tax Reduction Council, Memorandum to School Board, June 1921, SP, Folder "Tax Reduction Council." In 1915–1916 Seattle had 8 supervisors, compared with 52 in Pittsburg; 41 in Los Angeles; 37 in Boston; 29 in Cleveland; 28 in Rochester. See *Seattle School Bulletin*, June 1920, p. 4. In Tyack, *The One Best System* (p. 185), the total supervisory staff in 1920 was 159 in Boston; 329 in Detroit; 159 in Cleveland; 268 in Philadelphia. In Cubberley, *School Organization and Administration* (p. 39), Seattle ranks near the bottom in number of supervisors.

The TRC charged: "The teachers say they are supervised to death." Further, they pronounced that "supervision in the High Schools is not necessary. A teacher should be judged by the Principal of the school and by the ability of the pupils of the teacher to continue their work in more advanced courses and at the different universities." The TRC saw no reason for assistant superintendents or supervisors, especially since all had been out of the classroom for years. If they were also teachers, the TRC mused, "perhaps they would not ask such ridiculous and unproductive impossibilities of the class room teacher."[17]

In Cooper's view, the Seattle schools were strong owing to classroom-level administrators—the supervisors and department chairmen. Their continuing tasks were to set the standards high for teachers, to promote the standardized curriculum, and to see that faculty taught "the Seattle way." Curriculum and pedagogy were the glue that held together a growing district, full of new employees. The supervisors tried to ensure some measure of continuity and quality across the city. An article in the *Seattle School Bulletin* defended the supervisors, arguing that without them, "interest would slacken, unity would be wanting, and the work would get out of date and behind the times. Somebody particularly qualified and particularly interested is needed to keep up morale and progression."[18] The TRC felt that principals could and should do this work. The TRC perceived teachers as able to absorb a larger teaching load with less administrative overhead. What to the TRC looked like a way to lower cost was perceived by Cooper as an attack on his attempts to maintain quality.

The TRC often bitterly protested its inability to obtain reliable information from the superintendent's office, or to get people within the district to criticize the system honestly. The TRC blamed Cooper for being uncooperative, suggesting that he intimidated teachers and administration so that no one was willing to criticize. They claimed that the "MUTUAL ADMIRATION BOND" between Cooper and certain "favored so-called 'educators'" was such that the latter re-

17. Tax Reduction Council, Memorandum to School Board, July 1921, SP, Folder "Tax Reduction Council."
18. *Seattle School Bulletin*, June 1920, p. 3.

sented "constructive criticism as an attack upon 'Holier than Holy of Holies.' "[19]

In July 1921 Carl Croson, the man who had defeated Richard Winsor, raised the question of whether to continue the "social welfare work that is now being done by the School district, which is properly a matter of state, county and city work." The next week the board agreed to reduce activities "outside of strictly educational lines." Croson's motion consisted in part of a statement which Cooper and other progressives would have applauded up to the final words, but which in the context of the conservative reaction against progressive era schooling, stood as an indictment: "Whereas, Practically all of these lines of welfare work are primarily of a social nature, for the benefit of the whole of the social life of the city and county, particularly those lines of activity in connection with the care and support of delinquent, defective and unfortunate cases—properly belonging to state and county, and not to the School district."[20] The board appointed members Claude Eckart and Henry B. King to work with Croson to decide social welfare cuts.

The specific question for the committee was whether schools were the proper agency to fund and provide such services as health care, reduced-price food and milk, vocational counseling, speech therapists, special education teachers, parental schools, and teachers for the Children's Orthopedic Hospital. Should urban schools provide only an academic education for those who wanted and could succeed at it? Or should the system be concerned about all aspects of the welfare of all children?

Cooper, like most progressive era educators, had chosen the latter. He saw the schools as the logical delivery system for social welfare services. Within the board and administration, however, there had been different kinds of progressives. Like their counterparts elsewhere, some progressives had been less interested in humanitarian concerns and more interested in measures of efficiency, or in administrative reorganization, or in using schools as agencies of social policy. Each social welfare program had been debated between

19. Tax Reduction Council, Report on Seattle Public Schools Medical Department, 1921, SP, Folder "Tax Reduction Council."
20. Minutes of Board, July 1, 1921 (Croson); ibid., July 8, 1921 (motion).

contending views of "by what authority" a school system should be run: the health and welfare of the students; the cost-analysis of the program and whether the board wanted to fund it; or the legal basis for doing something with public money. What the 1920s conservatives attacked looked like a unified program only from the vantage point of the 1920s.

On July 22 the committee reported in favor of keeping most social welfare programs. They argued that it was cheaper to do so through the schools than through other agencies. Nonetheless, they now set up the budget in two categories, with one labeled "social welfare." This was the beginning of the end. Once programs Cooper thought integral to schooling were singled out, and once the public separated "basic education" from "social welfare," then the pressure to cut would be turned on the latter as an appendage.

At the end of July 1921, the board cut back the medical department. Dr. Ira C. Brown's salary was cut, Dr. Maybelle Parks was dropped, and the nurses were reduced from twenty-four to ten. Dr. Brown immediately resigned in protest. The TRC had advocated these cuts in the medical department. The TRC acknowledged that the medical department had "accomplished results in the prevention of sickness, infectious and contagious diseases and the spread of same," but they thought the department was too large. All those nurses were not needed because of the "general good health of our scholars," due to "our healthful and invigorating climate." By fall 1921 the Red Cross had assumed funding of a drastically reduced medical department, and Dr. Brown had returned.[21]

Cooper and the TRC engaged in a two-year battle over what it should cost to educate Seattle students. The TRC charged that teaching loads were too low. There were too many administrators along with too large a building program. Cooper justified the expenses because of heavy increases in the number of students and the length of time they stayed in school, and because Seattle had an exemplary, high-quality school system. This debate produced long, detailed reports from the TRC which put Cooper on the defensive. Eventually

21. Tax Reduction Council, Report on Seattle Public Schools Medical Department, 1921, SP, Folder "Tax Reduction Council."

the ways to reduce expenses were made quite clear by the TRC: either reduce by cutting salaries, or reduce by cutting programs.

The TRC claimed it was not out to destroy good schools, but that it favored good schools in which "education should be made pleasant." They wanted the schools to continue providing free textbooks. They supported the special education classes for "mental, moral and physical cripples." In good egalitarian fashion, they asserted that "all children without exception—rich or poor, noble or common— should have schooling and all should learn to the limit of their possibilities."[22] But the TRC wanted to cut expenses that they thought did not improve classroom instruction. They advocated cutting the salaries and jobs of administrators, raising the class size of high school teachers, and initially not cutting teacher salaries.

The effort to reduce expenses revolved around the question of teacher salaries. Ideologically conservative tax-cutting groups wanted schools to reduce expenses primarily by reducing programs and increasing the teaching load. Fiscal conservatives, such as Ebenezer Shorrock, wanted to continue programs but cut salaries. The choice would determine the kind of education offered and the kinds of students likely to attend. Should the board run a scaled-down school system, centered on the small classroom with adequately paid teachers, but with a high student dropout rate, and with those students needing social and medical services probably not getting them? Or should the board run a full program, aimed at attracting and keeping a high percentage of children and youth, but with disgruntled teachers working at a low salary or with large classes?

In August 1921, exasperated by Cooper's lack of response to their cost-cutting proposals, the TRC advocated reducing teacher salaries. Of teachers, they concluded that "surely there is nowhere else in the world so privileged a working class of folk." They criticized teachers for working during vacation, "which we have repeatedly been informed is needed for rest to make the teacher fit for work in the fall."[23]

22. Ibid.
23. Ibid., "Supplementary Grade School Report," August 1921, SP, Folder "Tax Reduction Council."

In the critics' view, expenditures could be reduced by decreasing the number of faculty (thereby increasing the class size), or by reorganizing the way students were taught. Secondary school teachers taught five sixty-minute periods per day. The TRC advocated eight forty-five-minute periods, with each teacher teaching seven periods. They claimed this would reduce—by anywhere from sixty to seventy-five—the number of teachers needed. The seven periods would require six hours per day in the classroom. "Surely," noted the TRC, "this is not an unreasonable amount of labor."[24]

Arguments over teaching loads, expenditures, and the quality of high school education revolved in the summer of 1921 around a method of teaching called "supervised study." Supervised study and the five-period day had been started in 1915–1916, enabling students to take four classes instead of three double-period classes. The first forty minutes of the hour were for recitation; the remainder were for supervised study. The teacher worked with students individually. Cooper said, "Each pupil's problem is worked out with him individually as far as possible, and is not permitted to interfere with the work of the class as a whole."[25]

The TRC proposed a shift to eight periods and the elimination of supervised study. The TRC called supervised study a fad promoted by Assistant Superintendent Thomas Cole, whom they accused of trying "to make it succeed at any cost, and, indeed, at all costs, by a continual 'simplifying' of the courses of study." As ideological conservatives, the TRC did not like individualized instruction. A student was to thrive or fail with group instruction, without class time reduced for personal help. They claimed that supervised study required one-fourth more teachers than did their proposed eight-period day. Furthermore, they blamed it for the "very great deterioration in the standards of scholarship in all high school studies." The TRC charged that "the instruction of the standard and difficult subjects, where thorough work cannot be replaced by camouflage, has become a farce." The percentage of "Ds" and failures had been greater at Broadway High School than in previous years. The Broad-

24. Ibid., Memorandum to School Board, August 1921, SP, Folder "Tax Reduction Council."
25. *Annual Report*, 1915–1916, p. 108.

way mathematics department was described as having undergone a "complete collapse," with "teachers who have resigned rather than see their work deteriorate and become a farce," and others "most unhappy over the situation."[26] It had reached the point where businesses were complaining about recent graduates, necessitating a proficiency test in commercial arithmetic for graduating seniors.

The TRC also advocated increasing class size, arguing that Cooper had kept it wastefully low. The TRC proposed average high-school class size of "35 or more." In the first semester of 1920–1921 at Broadway High School, the TRC reported that class size averaged: art, 14; manual arts, 17; science, 20; domestic science, 21; foreign languages, 21; history, 24; english and math, 25; and commercial, 27. According to district statistics, the average class size at one high school in 1920–1921 was 22.8 pupils, with 105 classes numbering under 20 pupils. Assistant Superintendent Cole told the TRC that he expected to absorb the next year's increase of 1,000 to 1,200 students by increasing class size. This "proved" to the TRC that classes were too small. They concluded by wryly noting: "Our school officials have evidently changed the old saying of 'Nothing too good' to 'Nothing too expensive' for Seattle Schools."[27]

Cooper was close to resigning as superintendent, but, as he had done throughout his tenure, he again defended teachers by countering the assertion that teachers could "do more" without sacrificing the quality of their teaching. Cooper, not apologizing for the expense of teaching well, argued that neither teaching nor learning would be as good under an eight-period day. Such a plan, he said, would put "an additional and excessive tax upon the teacher, limiting efficiency and producing irritation and bringing her at each day's end to the point of exhaustion."

Cooper further argued that the opening and closing of each class period

> call for considerable expenditure of energy in the successful conduct of a recitation. . . . There is considerable more draft upon the

26. Tax Reduction Council, Memorandum to School Board, August 1921, SP, Folder "Tax Reduction Council."
27. Ibid.

161

physical and mental force of the teacher from having to start seven times a day than only five. The increase in the number of pupils per teacher from 130 to about 200 makes 50 percent additional demand upon the nerve force of the teacher. . . . It increases by 50 percent the amount of written work to be examined. This means either a neglect to give such work or unending weariness and distaste.

Additionally, an eight-period plan would require that a teacher float from room to room, the effect of which would be "trying to equanimity and poise." Finally, Cooper argued that the periods at the end of the day are "the lean periods by reason of the fact that the students may be tiring and it is hard for them to give attention." And the teacher "is very likely to come to the last period without that buoyancy and intensity which is so much required in teaching that avails much."[28]

On March 17, 1922, Frank Cooper resigned, effective August 1, although he went on leave in mid-June. His resignation was not a surprise, given the attack from tax-cutting groups and a board no longer in sympathy with his vision of schooling. Ebenezer Shorrock noted that the board had known for some time that the sixty-seven-year-old Cooper was thinking of retiring. Immediately the TRC asked the board to delay choosing a new superintendent until after the May board election, presumably so that two more board members sympathetic to the TRC could be elected. But the board did not wait, and on March 31, 1922, it promoted Assistant Superintendent Thomas Cole to the job. The TRC was not pleased. They announced they would begin investigating all aspects of the school system.

Even while Cooper was trying to ward off the eight-period proposal, the TRC and others launched a drive to cut teacher salaries. The TRC wanted reduced by one-fourth all raises granted since January 1918. The four years since, they charged, had witnessed "a general scramble among the teachers of the various grades and high schools for higher salaries and still higher salaries, and your honorable body

28. Frank Cooper, Memorandum to School Board, March 3, 1922, SP, Folder "Tax Reduction Council."

seemed to agree that they were entitled to practically every demand they made." In March 1922 the board received many letters and petitions asking that teachers not be given a raise for the following year. Petitions for salary cuts came from many grade school PTAs and from the Federation of Women's Clubs. The economic strain produced by the Seattle recession was showing, and traditionally supportive PTA groups had now caught the tax-cutting fever. The TRC challenged the board and Cooper, saying, "Unless you cut these salaries to a point based upon present economic conditions, the Tax Reduction Council intends to keep up the fight, for we are satisfied that it is futile to reduce taxes in other channels while the salaries of teachers remain at the peak."[29]

The May 1922 election was the first school board election held jointly with the municipal election. The voter turnout dwarfed the numbers attracted by previous school elections. A socially prominent physician, Caspar W. Sharples, won one seat. Sharples rallied the old prewar progressives with a "no reductions" platform. For the other seat, Claude Eckart, a plumbing and heating contractor who had been appointed in January to replace George H. Walker, was defeated by tax-cutter E. F. Taylor, a former teacher and superintendent currently working as a publisher's agent.

After the election, with Cooper a lame duck, the tax-cutters sensed victory and showed great interest in the 1922–1923 budget. Citizens were invited to a meeting to comment on cutting the budget. After a number of speakers had talked about eliminating "frills," Ebenezer Shorrock replied that there were few frills in the system and that the saving from cutting them "would be relatively very small." Furthermore, he did not think economies should come at the expense of children. One of the mothers stated her support of Shorrock: "If the mothers of the District were asked where a cut should be made it would be found that they are unanimous in their demand that it be not made by cutting out the so-called 'frills.'" Mary A. Blair spoke of the poverty she had found as a school census taker. She stated emphatically that "here will be found mothers who

29. Tax Reduction Council, Memorandum to School Board, March 30, 1922, SP, Folder "Tax Reduction Council."

will not join in the demand for expenditure that helps to bring about such conditions."[30]

In one of his last memoranda to the board, Frank Cooper defended the high quality of the existing system. In the context of 1922, all that the prewar progressives had created was coming under serious attack and had to be justified to exist. New board member E. F. Taylor, tax-cutting opponent of Cooper, had claimed that the budget for 1922–1923 could be cut $500,000 without cutting teachers' salaries very much. Cooper agreed that it was indeed possible to cut $500,000, and he described the effects of such a budget curtailment.

Cooper listed cuts that could "save" $500,000. The cuts would eliminate two assistant superintendents; all directors and supervisors; all the attendance, part-time, and vocational guidance people; evening schools; kindergartens; classes for subnormal, deaf, blind, and near-blind children; and all free textbooks and supplies. They would also either reduce the salaries of teachers and principals, or reduce their numbers. Having listed ways to gut the system, Cooper declared: "All of this is quite possible. It is also very impossible from the standpoint of anyone who is deeply interested in the welfare of children and who consider their interests above that of politics or self. It is also quite impossible from the point of view of a great majority of the people of this city, who have children to be educated in the public schools."

Cooper charged the tax-cutters with abandoning those people who needed the benefits of a humane and progressive school system. He viewed the conservative tax cutters as elitists, willing to abandon those who needed extra help or services in order to save on school taxes. "I also stand and have stood for twenty-one years" said Cooper, "for the people who live here, for the people who want service for their children, for the many who have children they wish to have well taught, not for the few who must be given places whether or no. Mr. Taylor stands for the one in forty. I stand for the forty rather than for the one." Cooper concluded by noting that Caspar W. Sharples had just been elected to the board on a "no reduc-

30. Minutes of Board, May 26, 1922.

tion" platform, "and therefore the majority was not demanding that the Seattle Schools be dismantled."[31]

The board did not take Frank Cooper's advice. They cut the budget further on June 9, 1922. They reduced teachers' salaries by $150 per year; they eliminated evening schools, special schools, and schools for the deaf and blind; they cut supervisors, reduced clerks, and dropped some teachers; and they purchased no new textbooks or supplies. Cooper went on leave until his formal retirement in August. The new conservatives had clearly taken control of "his" school system. He moved to Marcroft Farm in Lake Forest Park, a suburb north of the city. Frank Cooper died there at age seventy-five on November 23, 1930.

31. Frank Cooper, Memorandum to School Board, June 2, 1922, SP, Folder "Budget."

10

The Triumph of Efficiency, 1922–1930

If Frank Cooper's pre–World War I school system seems distant today, it is worth noting that it also seemed remote to the Seattle school board and superintendent in the mid-1920s. Although most of the Cooper-era programs remained intact, new efficiency measures altered the purposes of schooling and the spirit of administration. Unlike the Cooper years, schooling now followed the dictates of scientific, efficient management.

The dominant themes of the 1920s in the Seattle schools were the main themes found in other leading urban school districts: an efficiency-minded, hierarchical administration using new tools (e.g., testing); a new structure (e.g., junior high schools); an expanded, diversified curriculum (e.g., different tracks, ability grouping); and the popular extracurriculum (e.g., sports, clubs, publications) to operate schools that were enrolling and graduating ever-increasing numbers of students.[1]

Cooper's successor, Thomas Cole, was superintendent from 1922–1930. Compared with Cooper, Cole better resembled the twentieth-century superintendent, as profiled in *Managers of Virtue* (Tyack and Hansot). Or, to apply categories from *The One Best System* (Tyack), Cole was "an administrative progressive," interested in control of schooling by a "centralized board and expert superintendent under a corporate model of governance," and with a differentiated curriculum that would lead to social efficiency and control.

1. See Tyack and Hansot, *Managers of Virtue*; Tyack, *The One Best System*. See also Joel Spring, *Education and the Rise of the Corporate State* (Boston: Beacon Press, 1972); Callahan, *Education and the Cult of Efficiency*; Krug, *The Shaping of the American High School*, vol. 2.

Cooper, by contrast, had been "a pedagogical progressive," who "took the hierarchical structure of differentiated schooling as a given and concentrated on inspiring the teacher to change her philosophy, her curriculum, and her methods in the classroom."[2]

As one of his first acts, Cole established a Department of Research headed by Fred C. Ayer of the University of Washington. With Ayer doing the statistical work, almost all aspects of school policy were now analyzed quantitatively. For example, using Ayer's 1924 curriculum study, the board proudly noted that, compared with students in other cities, Seattle students spent more time on "fundamental" subjects and less on "special" subjects, such as music, industrial arts, drawing, or physical education.[3] Cooper had not distinguished between fundamental and special subjects, preferring to view music, art, industrial arts, and physical education as part of the basic curriculum. Hence, Taylorism influenced schooling in a way it had never done during the Cooper years.

Cole, Ayer, and a fiscally conservative board reduced the cost of schooling per child, reduced the cost and scale of administration, and increased the size of high school classes. Per-pupil expenses had peaked in Cooper's last year. Then, despite a high bonded indebtedness, the cost per capita actually went down because the assessed valuation within the city went down. The board was proud that by 1927 Seattle was twenty-fourth among northern cities in cost per child, but eleventh in the percentage devoted to instruction.[4]

2. Tyack, *The One Best System*, pp. 196–97.

3. The Department of Research was established in October 1922. Ayer's first report is found in *Triennial Report*, 1921–1924, part 2; for board comments, see ibid., p. 51 (fundamental and special subjects).

4. Cole wrote that, from 1922 to 1929, "the schools have increased in attendance more than 25 percent during this 8-year period, while the expenditure for administration has decreased 13 percent" (*Triennial Report*, 1927–1930, p. 119). The budget percentage spent for administration between 1922–1929 went from 3.46% to 3.0%, while the percentage spent on instruction went from 68.41% to 72.68% (*Triennial Report*, 1927–1930, p. 119). Total school costs peaked in 1921, reaching $101 per capita in grade and $149 per capita in high schools. In 1927 the district spent $85 per capita in grade and $117 per capita in high schools. According to U.S. Bureau of Education data, Seattle ranked 24th in per capita expense in 1927, but 11th in percentage devoted to instruction (as reported in *Triennial Report*, 1924–1927, pp. 18–20).

Administration had been cut, and the overall expenditure had been cut. The tax reduction groups had won.

The school's role toward young adolescents provides another indicator of the change between the Cooper era and the 1920s. During the Cole years, student enrollment (especially among adolescents) continued to grow at a faster rate than the city's population. In other words, more students were staying in school for more years. To respond to enrollment pressure in the 1920s with the pre–World War I pattern would have meant building more small grade schools and more high schools. Cole and the board thought this unnecessarily expensive, especially at a time of political cries for lowering taxes. Instead, they favored building junior high schools, touted as a less expensive way for a school system to grow.[5]

Adolescent enrollment pressure was not the only reason for junior highs. Cooper had wanted young adolescents kept in small neighborhood grade schools, where people knew them well and they were taught by only a few adults. The 1920s educators complained about Cooper's small grade schools, none of which exceeded twenty rooms, compared with twenty-four to thirty-six rooms typical elsewhere. A 1923 report concluded that Seattle had "too many school units," blaming Seattle's "peculiar conditions" of hills, water, and the resulting neighborhood pressure for schools.[6] Ignored were Cooper's reasons for small schools through grade eight, having to do with needs of the developing children.

Cole recommended larger schools, because they "prove more economical from the point of view of maintenance and operation." The 1920s educators also complained about the inadequacy of industrial training—which only existed in half of the grade schools (those large enough to have a shop and a teacher). Cole thought the junior

---

5. For a graph comparing Seattle school enrollment with population growth, see *Triennial Report*, 1921–1924, p. 8. For a graph showing percentage increase in grade, intermediate, and high-school enrollments, 1910–1923, see ibid., p. 9. Average daily attendance in 1921 was 41,385—in 1927 it was 51,046. Between 1917–1927, average daily attendance increased 57 percent (ibid., 1924–1927, p. 2). In advocating junior high schools, Cole cited "needs of individual pupils" and a "wider selection of subjects," adding that "larger schools likewise mean reduced costs" (ibid., pp. 22-23).

6. *Triennial Report*, 1921–1924, pp. 30-31.

high "offers eventually the best solution of our rather top-heavy building arrangement."[7] With the junior high's diverse curriculum, the use of intelligence tests, ability grouping, and guidance counselors, these young adolescents could begin to sort themselves into appropriate life paths.

Junior high advocates pointed to better facilities and specialized faculty in large junior high schools. When they talked about the needs of the adolescents, they pointed to curricular choices ("wider selection of subjects, including manual training and home economics"), and better trained subject specialists ("required to be college or university graduates"). They talked about junior highs as places where "the needs of individual pupils could be met more effectively," and where pupils grouped by ability could "discover interests and capacities" with the help of guidance counselors who could give "careful advisement in the selection of elective subjects." The seventh and eighth grades in a junior high building were considered "mainly try-out years." Among themselves, the board talked about junior highs as a way to save money: "Larger schools mean reduced costs."[8] This efficient approach to early adolescence was very different from what Cooper had advocated.

The first two junior high schools, Alexander Hamilton and John Marshall, were completed for fall 1927. Unlike most grade schools, their names did not represent neighborhoods. By 1930 half of the students in grades seven, eight, and nine attended junior high schools.[9]

For the school board, efficiency was uppermost in the 1920s in a way it had not been for Cooper before World War I. The board and Cole were interested in the most efficient ways to move large numbers of students through the system and, in the process, prepare them for their adult roles. All elementary pupils were now given intelligence tests and were taught some subjects by ability grouping. Both had been resisted in the Cooper years. Starting in 1927, all grade schools used a semidepartmental plan, an organizational plan

7. Ibid., p. 27; ibid., p. 30.
8. Ibid., 1924–1927, pp. 22-23.
9. Ibid., 1927–1930, p. 115.

adapted from the "platoon system" of Gary, Indiana.[10] In semi-departmental grade schools, students left their regular teacher for part of a day to see specialist teachers in reading, shop, science, music, or physical education. While such a plan had existed at Green Lake School since 1917, Cooper had opposed expanding this experiment to other grade schools.

The 1920s emphasis on efficiency also changed high schools. Beginning with a modest trial in Cooper's last year, ability grouping quickly spread to become the norm in Seattle high schools by 1925. To keep up with enrollment pressure, the board raised class size in high school, sharply reducing the number of classes under twenty students. In an effort to relieve overcrowding by adding more class sections, two high schools in 1926–1927 scrapped Cooper's "supervised study" (five periods of seventy minutes) in favor of six one-hour periods, with one a study hall.[11]

Efficiency meant that some programs had to be all or partially self-supporting. The school clinic was paid for by patient fees and the Junior Red Cross. Night school was reinstated, but was reduced from ten to three schools. Starting in 1922–1923, tuition was charged to make the night school self-supporting. Night school shifted away from being an adult's second chance at grade school or high school classes to being more of an adult vocational school..

Administration was reduced by dropping supervisors and others concerned with curriculum. Between 1922–1929, student attendance increased by 25 percent, while the amount spent on administration was reduced by 13 percent, down to 3 percent of the total budget.[12] With only a few supervisors, the principal's task of evaluating and rating teachers was given a new seriousness, starting in 1925–1926 with an elaborate quantified scheme for evaluating teachers.

In the Cooper era, subject-matter supervisors had visited teachers and promoted "the Seattle way" to teach. This had been the glue

10. See Ronald Cohen and Raymond Mohl, *The Paradox of Progressive Education: The Gary Plan and Urban Schooling* (Port Washington, N.Y.: Kennikat Press, 1979); see also *Triennial Report*, 1924–1927, pp. 23–27.

11. *Triennial Report*, 1921–1924, p. 79 (ability grouping). In one high school, the average class size went from 22.8 in 1920, to 24.4 in 1924; and the number of classes with less than twenty students went from 105 in 1920, to 69 in 1924 (ibid., p.77).

12. *Triennial Report*, 1927–1930, p. 119.

that bonded together disparate parts of the school system: teachers recruited from all over the United States, and widely scattered buildings in new neighborhoods. That glue was watered down in the 1920s. Supplanting the roving supervisors, Summit School was established in 1926 as a demonstration school, to which teachers came to observe curriculum and methods. Indeed, itinerant supervisors maintaining quality control and promoting good teaching might not have been as necesssary in the 1920s as in the formative Cooper years.

The overall program of the Cooper era remained. There still were special education classes (for the retarded, speech-impaired, deaf, and blind), boys' and girls' parental schools, opportunity classes, part-time classes, teachers at Children's Orthopedic Hospital and the juvenile detention center, summer vacation schools, evening schools, and a school medical clinic. None of the second-chance and social welfare programs were cut. Rather, the emphasis on curriculum was reduced, and a new emphasis on efficient use of every space was included. The dominant themes in urban education were tracking, testing, guidance counseling, junior high schools, vocational education, and large schools—all in the name of efficiency in response to steady increases in enrollment.

The schools of the 1920s emphasized efficiency at the expense of small schools, the conditions of teaching (class size, overall teaching load), and the pedagogical emphasis on learning as inquiry. It was not inevitable that the purposes of Cooper's system had to change, even as it grew in enrollment. Progressives, labor, Socialists, and prominent women's groups had built a system which had kept large-scale urban schooling as a collection of human-scale units.

With the war and its subsequent political and economic dislocations, the de facto coalition of progressive-spirited groups came apart for reasons having to do with wartime patriotism. If the lack of pro-war enthusiasm from Socialists, unions, and progressive educators made them appear unpatriotic to politically conservative people, then progressive school policies were likewise considered suspect. Prewar progressives were swept out of power for financial and ideological reasons ("Spend less, do less."), and with them went their vision of schooling.

The fiscally and ideologically conservative (and patriotic) men who controlled the Seattle schools in the 1920s poured their new wine of efficiency into Cooper's old bottles. They offered fewer services to students, saved money by increasing class size and teaching loads, and increased the guidance and sorting functions of the school. This alteration of Cooper's system did not result in a bad school system. Indeed, judging from the outward appearance of the Seattle schools in the 1920s, it looked like a larger version of Cooper's system. But the purposes and spirit were clearly different.

The public school system built by Frank Cooper remained unchanged in its outward structure until the 1960s. From the early twentieth century until the 1960s was a long run for an institution as vulnerable to change as public schooling. Its longevity was especially notable because critical policy decisions had been made quickly under the pressure of Seattle's rapid transformation into a brand-new city.

Seattle did not develop as a later copy of eastern and midwestern cities. Neither did the Seattle schools develop according to the patterns found in any other city. The combination of Seattle's newness as a city, its demographic mix, its geography, and its progressive leadership resulted in a school system which was a variation on themes found nationally.

In a 1919 memorandum, Cooper had expressed the relationship between his tenure and the development of the new Seattle. He wrote: "The wide-awake citizen knows that clean, finely lighted streets, pure water, ample and effective fire and police protection, miles of scenic boulevards and numerous beautiful parks are civic assets and furnish an indirect contribution to the profitableness of business." But good schools exceeded even these attributes: "To have it said of a city that its chief pride is in providing adequately for the education of its youth outweighs all the others in both general and particular effects."[13]

What made the Seattle school system work well, well enough to thrive for decades, was Frank Cooper's vision of schooling. Regardless of changing board politics in subsequent decades, Cooper's

13. Frank Cooper, Memorandum to School Board, April 17, 1919, SP, Folder "Salaries."

persistent understanding of "good schools" rang true with many people. Cooper shaped his generation's institutional answers to enduring school questions about money, control, and purpose. He did not apologize for the cost of "good schools." Cooper envisioned urban grade schools as small, humane places where staff really knew the children and their families; and grade and high schools as places to make all children and adolescents literate, knowledgeable, and civil. His vision included a traditional liberal arts curriculum, enriched with lessons from real life, and taught with a variety of methods; high schools and night schools with open doors, offering second chances at education for adolescents and adults; and a social welfare aspect to schooling, so that the life-chances of a child were not significantly reduced by hunger, poverty, or poor health. He envisioned all schools with a fundamental emphasis on the conditions under which good teaching could occur. All of these characteristics were—and still are—the basic and enduring ingredients of "good schools."

Bibliography

Manuscript Collections

Seattle. Seattle Public Schools Archives. Superintendent's Papers.
Seattle. University of Washington Libraries. Thomas Burke Papers.

Newspapers

Argus, 1901–1922.
Seattle Times, 1901–1922.
Seattle Union Record, 1901–1922.

Books

Ayer, Fred C. *Studies In Administrative Research*. 2 vols. Seattle: Board of Directors, Seattle Public Schools, 1924.
Bagley, Clarence. *A History of Seattle from the Earliest Settlement to the Present Time*. Chicago: S. J. Clarke Publishing Co., 1916.
Best, John Hardin, ed. *Historical Inquiry in Education: A Research Agenda*. Washington, D.C.: American Educational Research Association, 1983.
Bowles, Samuel, and Gintis, Herbert. *Schooling in Capitalist America. Educational Reform and the Contradictions of Economic Life*. New York: Basic Books, 1976.
Briggs, Thomas H. *The Junior High School*. Boston: Houghton Mifflin Co., 1920.
Callahan, Raymond E. *Education and the Cult of Efficiency*. Chicago: University of Chicago Press, 1962.

Bibliography

Cavallo, Dominick. *Muscles and Morals: Organized Playgrounds and Urban Reform, 1880–1920*. Philadelphia: University of Pennsylvania Press, 1981.

Church, Robert, and Sedlak, Michael. *Education in the United States: An Interpretative History*. New York: Free Press, 1976.

Clark, Norman. *Mill Town: A Social History of Everett, Washington, from Its Earliest Beginnings on the Shores of Puget Sound to the Tragic and Infamous Event Known as the Everett Massacre*. Seattle: University of Washington Press, 1970.

——————. *Washington: A Bicentennial History*. New York: W. W. Norton & Co., 1976.

Coffman, Lotus Delta. *The Social Composition of the Teaching Population*. New York: Teachers College, Columbia University, 1911.

Cohen, Ronald, and Mohl, Raymond. *The Paradox of Progressive Education: The Gary Plan and Urban Schooling*. Port Washington, N.Y.: Kennikat Press, 1979.

Commission on the Reorganization of Secondary Education. *Cardinal Principles of Secondary Education*. Washington, D.C.: Government Printing Office, 1918.

Committee of Ten on Secondary School Studies. *Report*. New York: National Education Association, American Book Company, 1894.

Counts, George S. *The Selective Character of American Secondary Education*. Chicago: University of Chicago Press, 1922.

Craven, Hermon W. *Report of Hermon W. Craven on the Teaching of United States History in the Grammar Schools*. Seattle: Board of Directors, Seattle Public Schools, 1913.

Cremin, Lawrence. *The Transformation of the School: Progressivism in American Education, 1876–1957*. New York: Random House, 1961.

Cuban, Larry. *How Teachers Taught: Constancy and Change in American Classrooms, 1890–1980*. New York: Longman, 1984.

Cubberley, Ellwood P. *Changing Conceptions of Education*. Boston: Houghton Mifflin Co., 1909.

——————. *The Portland Survey: A Textbook on City School Administration Based on a Concrete Study*. Yonkers-on-Hudson, N.Y.: World Book Co., 1915.

——————. *Public School Administration: A Statement of the Fundamental Principles Underlying the Organization and Administration of Public Education*. Boston: Houghton Mifflin Co., 1916.

——————. *School Organization and Administration: A Concrete Study Based on the Salt Lake City School Survey*. Yonkers-on-Hudson, N.Y.: World Book Co., 1916.

175

Bibliography

Dewey, John. *The Child and the Curriculum*. Chicago: University of Chicago Press, 1902.

──────. *The Educational Situation*. Chicago: University of Chicago Press, 1902.

──────. *Moral Principles in Education*. Boston: Houghton Mifflin Co., 1909.

──────. *My Pedagogic Creed*. New York: E. L. Kellogg & Co., 1897.

──────. *The School and Society*. Chicago: University of Chicago Press, 1900.

Dworkin, Martin S., ed., *Dewey On Education*. New York: Teachers College Press, 1959.

Dykhuizen, George. *The Life and Mind of John Dewey*. Carbondale and Edwardsville: Southern Illinois University Press, 1973.

Eaton, William E. *The American Federation of Teachers, 1916–1961: A History of the Movement*. Carbondale and Edwardsville: Southern Illinois University Press, 1975.

Friedheim, Robert L. *The Seattle General Strike*. Seattle: University of Washington Press, 1964.

Gould, James E. *Planning and Improving School Grounds*. Seattle: County Superintendent of Schools, 1916.

Graham, Patricia Albjerg. *Progressive Education: From Arcady to Academe*. New York: Teachers College Press, 1967.

──────. *Community and Class in American Education, 1865–1918*. New York: Wiley, 1974.

Gribskov, Margaret. "Adelaide Pollock and the Founding of NCAWE." In *Women Educators: Employees of Schools in Western Countries*. Edited by Patricia A. Schmuck. New York: SUNY Press, 1987.

Grubb, W. Norton, and Lazerson, Marvin. *Broken Promises: How Americans Fail Their Children*. New York: Basic Books, 1982.

Hiner, N. Ray, and Hawes, Joseph M., eds. *Growing Up in America: Children in Historical Perspective*. Urbana: University of Illinois Press, 1985.

Hoag, Ernest B., and Terman, Lewis M. *Health Work in the Schools*. Boston: Houghton Mifflin Co., 1914.

Jensen, Joan M. *The Price of Vigilance*. Chicago: Rand McNally, 1968.

Kantor, Harvey, and Tyack, David, eds., *Work, Youth, and Schooling: Historical Perspectives on Vocationalism in American Education*. Stanford: Stanford University Press, 1982.

Karier, Clarence; Violas, Paul; and Spring, Joel. *Roots of Crisis: American Education in the Twentieth Century*. Chicago: Rand McNally, 1973.

176

Katz, Michael B. *Class, Bureaucracy and Schools: The Illusion of Educational Change in America.* New York: Praeger, 1975.

Kett, Joseph. *Rites of Passage: Adolescence in America, 1790 to the Present.* New York: Basic Books, 1977.

Kliebard, Herbert. *The Struggle For the American Curriculum, 1893–1958.* Boston: Routledge & Kegan Paul, 1986.

Kolko, Gabriel. *The Triumph of Conservatism: A Reinterpretation of American History, 1900–1916.* New York: Free Press of Glencoe, 1963.

Koos, Leonard V. *The Junior High School.* New York: Harcourt, Brace & Co., 1921.

Krug, Edward A. *The Shaping of the American High School.* 2 vols. New York: Harper & Row, 1964, 1972.

Lazerson, Marvin. *Origins of the Urban School: Public Education in Massachusetts, 1870–1915.* Cambridge, Mass.: Harvard University Press, 1971.

Lazerson, Marvin, and Grubb, W. Norton. *Vocationalism and American Education: A Documentary History, 1870–1970.* New York: Teachers College Press, 1974.

Lubove, Roy. *The Professional Altruist: The Emergence of Social Work as a Career, 1880–1930.* Cambridge, Mass.: Harvard University Press, 1965.

Miyamoto, Shotaro Frank. *Social Solidarity Among the Japanese in Seattle.* Seattle: University of Washington Press, 1939.

Nasaw, David. *Children of the City: At Work and at Play.* New York: Oxford University Press, 1985.

———. *Schooled To Order: A Social History of Public Schooling in the United States.* New York: Oxford University Press, 1979.

O'Connor, Harvey. *Revolution in Seattle: A Memoir.* New York: Monthly Review Press, 1964.

Peterson, H. C., and Fite, Gilbert. *Opponents of War, 1917–1918.* Madison: University of Wisconsin Press, 1957.

Peterson, Paul E. *The Politics of School Reform, 1870–1940.* Chicago: University of Chicago Press, 1985.

Platt, Anthony. *The Child Savers: The Invention of Delinquency.* Chicago: University of Chicago Press, 1977.

The Public School System of San Francisco, California. Washington, D.C.: United States Commissioner of Education, 1917.

Rapeer, Louis W. *School Health Administration.* New York: Teachers College, Columbia University, 1913.

Reed, Anna Yeomans. *Seattle Children in School and Industry, with Recommendations for Increasing the Efficiency of the School System and for Decreasing the*

Bibliography

Social and Economic Waste Incident to the Employment of Children 14 to 18 Years of Age. Seattle: Board of School Directors, Seattle Public Schools, 1915.

——————. *Vocational Guidance Report, 1913–1916.* Seattle: Board of Directors, Seattle Public Schools, 1916.

Reese, William J. *Power and the Promise of School Reform: Grass-roots Movements during the Progressive Era.* Boston: Routledge & Kegan Paul, 1986.

Reid, Robert L., ed. *Battleground: The Autobiography of Margaret A. Haley.* Urbana: University of Illinois Press, 1982.

Rules and Regulations. Seattle: Board of Directors, Seattle Public Schools, 1902.

Sale, Roger. *Seattle: Past to Present.* Seattle: University of Washington Press, 1976.

Schlossman, Steven L. *Love and the American Delinquent: The Theory and Practice of Progressive Juvenile Justice, 1825–1920.* Chicago: University of Chicago Press, 1977.

Schmid, Calvin. *Growth and Distribution of Minority Races in Seattle.* Seattle: Seattle Public Schools, 1964.

——————. *Social Trends in Seattle.* Seattle: University of Washington Press, 1944.

Schmid, Calvin; Nobbe, Charles; and Mitchell, Arlene. *Nonwhite Races, State of Washington.* Olympia: Washington State Planning and Community Affairs Agency, 1968.

Schwantes, Carlos A. *Radical Heritage: Labor, Socialism, and Reform in Washington and British Columbia, 1885–1917.* Seattle: University of Washington Press, 1979.

Sears, Jesse B.; and Henderson, Adin D. *Cubberley of Stanford and His Contribution to American Education.* Stanford: Stanford University Press, 1957.

A Seattle Legacy: The Olmsted Parks. Seattle: Seattle Department of Parks and Recreation, 1981.

Shannon, David. *The Socialist Party of America: A History.* New York: Macmillan Co., 1955.

Sizer, Theodore. *Secondary Schools at the Turn of the Century.* New Haven: Yale University Press, 1964.

Spring, Joel. *Education and the Rise of the Corporate State.* Boston: Beacon Press, 1972.

Strayer, George D. *Age and Grade Census of Schools and Colleges: A Study of Retardation and Elimination.* Washington, D.C.: United States Bureau of Education, 1911.

Strong, Anna Louise. *I Change Worlds: The Remaking of an American.* Seattle: Seal Press, 1979.

178

Strong, Tracy B., and Keyssar, Helene. *Right in Her Soul: The Life of Anna Louise Strong.* New York: Random House, 1983.

Taylor, Frederick W. *The Principles of Scientific Management.* New York: Harper & Brothers, 1911.

Terman, Lewis M. *The Hygiene of the School Child.* Boston: Houghton Mifflin Co., 1914.

——————. *The Intelligence of School Children.* Boston: Houghton Mifflin Co., 1919.

——————. *The Measurement of Intelligence.* Boston: Houghton Mifflin Co., 1916.

——————. *The Teacher's Health: A Study in the Hygiene of an Occupation.* Boston: Houghton Mifflin Co., 1913.

Terman, Lewis M.; Dickson, Virgil; Sutherland, A. H.; Franzen, Raymond; Tupper, C. R.; and Fernald, Grace. *Intelligence Tests and School Reorganization.* Yonkers-on-Hudson, N.Y.: World Book Co., 1923.

Troen, Selwyn. *The Public and the Schools: Shaping the St. Louis System, 1838–1920.* Columbia: University of Missouri Press, 1975.

Tyack, David. *The One Best System: A History of American Urban Education.* Cambridge, Mass.: Harvard University Press, 1974.

Tyack, David, and Hansot, Elisabeth. *Managers of Virtue: Public School Leadership in America, 1820–1980.* New York: Basic Books, 1982.

Tyor, Peter L., and Bell, Leland V. *Caring for the Retarded in America: A History.* Westport, Conn.: Greenwood Press, 1984.

Urban, Wayne. *Why Teachers Organized.* Detroit: Wayne State University Press, 1982.

VanDenburg, Joseph K. *The Junior High School Idea.* New York: Henry Holt & Co., 1922.

Wallin, J. E. Wallace. *The Education of Handicapped Children.* Boston: Houghton Mifflin Co., 1924.

Weinstein, James. *The Decline of Socialism in America, 1912–1925.* New York: Monthly Review Press, 1967.

——————. *The Corporate Ideal in the Liberal State, 1900–1918.* Boston: Beacon Press, 1968.

Wesley, Edgar B. *NEA—The First Hundred Years: The Building of the Teaching Profession.* New York: Harper & Row, 1957.

Wiebe, Robert H. *The Search For Order, 1877–1920.* New York: Hill and Wang, 1967.

Wirth, Arthur G. *Education in the Technological Society: The Vocational-Liberal Studies Controversy in the Early Twentieth Century.* Scranton, Penn.: Intext Educational Publishers, 1972.

Bibliography

Dissertations and Theses

Bardarson, Otto W. "A History of Elementary and Secondary Education in Seattle." M.A. thesis, University of Washington, 1928.

Blackburn, Richard L. "Federal Aid to Education in the State of Washington." M.A. thesis, University of Washington, 1925.

Cravens, Hamilton. "A History of the Washington Farmer-Labor Party, 1918–1924." M.A. thesis, University of Washington, 1962.

Dawson, Jan C. "A Social Gospel Portrait: The Life of Sydney Dix Strong, 1860–1938." M.A. thesis, University of Washington, 1972.

Jacoby, Daniel. "Schools, Unions, and Training: Seattle, 1900–1940." Ph.D. dissertation, University of Washington, 1986.

Kussick, Marilyn. "Social Reform as a Tool of Urban Reform: The Emergence of the Twentieth-Century Public School in Newark, New Jersey, 1890–1920." Ph.D. dissertation, Rutgers University, 1974.

Laing, James M. "A History of the Provision for Mentally Retarded Children in the State of Washington." Ed.D. dissertation, University of Washington, 1955.

Lash, Frederick M. "An Historical and Functional Study of Public Education in Seattle." Ph.D. dissertation, University of Washington, 1934.

MacDonald, Alexander N. "Seattle's Economic Development, 1880–1910." Ph.D. dissertation, University of Washington, 1959.

Miller, Carrie L. "The History of Education in Seattle." M.A. thesis, University of Washington, 1929.

Morris, Francis N. "A History of Teacher Unionism in the State of Washington, 1920–1945." M.A. thesis, University of Washington, 1969.

Ogle, Stephanie F. "Anna Louise Strong, Progressive and Propagandist." Ph.D. dissertation, University of Washington, 1981.

Pendergrass, Lee. "Urban Reform and Voluntary Association: A Case Study of the Seattle Municipal League, 1910–1929." Ph.D. dissertation, University of Washington, 1972.

Randall, Prudence B. "The Meaning of Progressivism in Urban School Reform: Cleveland, 1901–1909." Ph.D. dissertation, Case Western Reserve University, 1971.

Reiff, Janice L. "Urbanization and the Social Structure: Seattle, Washington, 1852–1910." Ph.D. dissertation, University of Washington, 1981.

Rockafellar, Nancy, "Public Health in Progressive Seattle, 1876–1919." M.A. thesis, University of Washington, 1986.

Roper, Marion W. "A Neighborhood Study of Juvenile Delinquency in Seattle." M.A. thesis, University of Washington, 1923.

Bibliography

Saltvig, Robert. "The Progressive Movement in Washington." Ph.D. dissertation, University of Washington, 1967.

Shradar, Victor L. "Ethnic Politics, Religion, and the Public Schools of San Francisco, 1849–1933." Ph.D. dissertation, Stanford University, 1974.

Tien, Joseleyne S. "The Educational Theories of American Socialists, 1900–1920." Ph.D. dissertation, Michigan State University, 1972.

Tjaden, Norman F. "Populists and Progressives of Washington: A Comparative Study." M.A. thesis, University of Washington, 1961.

Troth, Dennis C. "History and Development of Common School Legislation in Washington." Ph.D. dissertation, University of Washington, 1925.

Weiss, Nancy P. "Save the Children: A History of the Children's Bureau, 1903–1918." Ph.D. dissertation, University of California at Los Angeles, 1974.

Journal Articles

Cohen, Sol. "The Industrial Education Movement, 1906–1917." *American Quarterly* 20, no. 1 (Spring 1968): 95–110.

Cole, Thomas. "Segregation at the Broadway High School." *School Review* 23, no. 8 (October 1915): 550–54.

Everhart, Robert B. "From Universalism to Usurpation: An Essay on the Antecedents to Compulsory School Attendance Legislation." *Review of Educational Research* 47, no. 3 (Summer 1977): 499–530.

Graebner, William. "Retirement in Education: The Economic and Social Functions of the Teachers' Pension." *History of Education Quarterly* 18, no. 4 (Winter 1978): 397–417.

Hays, Samuel P. "The Politics of Reform in Municipal Government in the Progressive Era." *Pacific Northwest Quarterly* 55, no. 4 (October 1964): 157–69.

Hines, Harlan C. "The Education of Mental Defectives in the Public Schools of Seattle." *School and Society* 17, no. 426 (February 24, 1923): 216–21.

Lazerson, Marvin. "Urban Reform and the Schools: Kindergartens in Massachusetts, 1870–1915." *History of Education Quarterly* 11, no. 2 (Summer 1971): 115–37.

Murray, Keith. "The Charles Neiderhauser Case: Patriotism in the Seattle Schools, 1919." *Pacific Northwest Quarterly* 74, no. 1 (January 1983): 11–17.

Nearing, Scott. "Who's Who on Our Boards of Education." *School and Society* 5, no. 108 (January 20, 1917): 89–90.

Bibliography

O'Hanlon, Timothy. "Interscholastic Athletics, 1900–1940: Shaping Citizens for Unequal Roles in the Modern Industrial State." *Educational Theory* 30, no. 2 (Spring 1980): 89–103.

Reese, William J. "The Control of Urban School Boards During the Progressive Era: A Reconsideration." *Pacific Northwest Quarterly* 68, no. 4 (October 1977): 164–74.

——————. " 'Partisans of the Proletariat': The Socialist Working Class and the Milwaukee Schools, 1890–1920." *History of Education Quarterly* 21, no. 1 (Spring 1981): 3–50.

Rockafellar, Nancy. " 'In Gauze We Trust': Public Health and Spanish Influenza on the Home Front, Seattle, 1918–1919." *Pacific Northwest Quarterly* 77, no. 3 (July 1986): 104–13.

Rury, John L. "Vocationalism for Home and Work: Women's Education in the United States, 1880–1930." *History of Education Quarterly* 24, no. 1 (Spring 1984): 21–44.

Sedlak, Michael W. "Young Women and the City: Adolescent Deviance and the Transformation of Educational Policy, 1870–1960." *History of Education Quarterly* 23, no. 1 (Spring 1983): 1–28.

Tyack, David. "Pilgrim's Progress: Toward a Social History of the School Superintendency, 1860–1960." *History of Education Quarterly* 16, no. 3 (Fall 1976): 257–300.

——————. "Ways of Seeing: An Essay on the History of Compulsory Schooling." *Harvard Educational Review* 46, no. 3 (August 1976): 355–89.

Urban, Wayne. "Organized Teachers and Educational Reform During the Progressive Era, 1890–1920." *History of Education Quarterly* 16, no. 1 (Spring 1976): 35–52.

Index